AGATA TOROMANOFF

BEAUTIFUL ORDINARY OBJECTS

EVERYDAY LUXURY

SCHÖNE DINGE FÜR DEN ALLTAG

teNeues

SUMMARY
INHALTSVERZEICHNIS

INTRODUCTION

Many of us may feel like raising an eyebrow or cracking a smile at the sight of a paper clip, a bottle opener, or a ping-pong paddle sold at the same price as a top-brand handbag or a pair of luxury boots. These ordinary objects clad in the gloss of luxury will certainly remind the wisest among us of Andersen's fairy tale about the Emperor's new clothes and the excesses of naivety that vanity can lead to. And yet, we're already surrounded by "ordinary" luxury products in our everyday lives – watches, bags, scarves, and shoes, to name but a few. So why should we question other luxury objects that could embellish our everyday surroundings? Why couldn't we extend our love for beautiful things to simple, very useful objects, to our favourite games, even tic-tac-toe, or to our beloved pets?

While the lavish yet ordinary accessories featured in this book don't fit, at first glance, into our concept of luxury, their magnificent extravagance strikes us, halfway between a flash of genius and an epiphany, with a touch of madness. These objects, which we take for granted in normal life, suddenly shine with a thousand lights. And this is precisely the essence, and magic, of luxury: to sublimate, to transfigure everyday reality by offering products of a refinement unimaginable to simple mortals, to be a dream world that is both unaffordable to most of us and nevertheless made accessible and understandable. Just like poetry transforms ordinary words into gems, so do luxury brands with the objects they create. Much more than flashy, gaudy, gleaming cars, yachts, or other ostentatious symbols of luxury, these everyday objects reinterpreted by the world's finest brands bear witness to true refinement.

These products are not a slightly improved version of the basic ones, simply stamped with a prestigious brand name and wrapped in the glamour of luxury. The same spirit of perfection that drives the artistry behind haute couture, luxury leather goods, and jewellery is embodied in the making of these products. The same extreme attention to detail motivates product designers, craftspeople, and manufacturers to bring their creations up to the status of luxury items in their own right. This book takes you along on the fascinating quest for the perfect object, with designers uncompromisingly searching for the best materials, the best shapes, to offer nearly one-of-a-kind objects destined to be in daily use for decades and perhaps generations to come. It is a tribute to excellence and the extraordinary skills hidden in fairly ordinary objects. I am willing to bet that you will cover the pages of your own copy with post-it notes (deluxe or not – it doesn't matter!) as you imagine your daily life surrounded by these objects.

EINLEITUNG

Beim Anblick einer Büroklammer, eines Flaschenöffners oder eines Tischtennisschlägers, die zum gleichen Preis verkauft werden wie Luxus-Handtaschen oder -stiefel, zieht wohl so mancher von uns eine Augenbraue hoch oder grinst verstohlen. Solche gewöhnlichen Gegenstände, plötzlich in Luxus gehüllt, erinnern die Belesenen unter uns sicherlich an Andersens Märchen über des Kaisers neue Kleider und die Gefahren, die in der Eitelkeit lauern. Und doch sind wir in unserem Alltag bereits von „gewöhnlichen" Luxusprodukten umgeben – Uhren, Taschen, Schals und Schuhen, um nur einige zu nennen. Warum stellen wir also andere Luxusobjekte in Frage, die unsere alltägliche Umgebung verschönern können? Warum dehnen wir die Liebe zu schönen Dingen nicht auf schlichte Gebrauchsgegenstände aus, auf unsere Lieblingsspiele, auf ein simples Tic-Tac-Toe, oder auf unsere geliebten Haustiere?

Obgleich die gewöhnlichen, wenn auch noblen, Accessoires, die in diesem Buch vorgestellt werden, auf den ersten Blick nicht der landläufigen Auffassung von Luxus entsprechen, erscheint uns ihre überbordende Extravaganz doch als eine Mischung aus Geniestreich, Offenbarung und einem Hauch von Wahnsinn. Die Gegenstände, die wir normalerweise für selbstverständlich halten, funkeln mit einem Mal leuchtend hell. Und genau dies ist die Quintessenz, die Magie wahren Luxus: ganz normale Menschen erhalten Zugang zu Produkten unvorstellbarer Finesse, die den Alltag erhabener werden lassen. Luxus erscheint uns als Traumwelt: einerseits für die meisten von uns unerschwinglich, andererseits jedoch begreifbar gemacht und im Rahmen des Möglichen. Auf die gleiche Weise, wie Poesie gewöhnliche Worte in Juwelen verwandelt, verfahren auch Luxusmarken mit den Objekten, die sie erschaffen. Mehr noch als glänzende, protzige Autos, Yachten oder andere auffällige Luxussymbole zeugen diese Neuinterpretationen alltäglicher Gegenstände, erdacht von den besten Marken der Welt, von echter Kunstfertigkeit.

Bei diesen Produkten handelt es sich nicht einfach um die leicht verbesserte Ausführung der Basisversion, die durch einen prestigeträchtigen Markennamen in luxuriösen Glamour gehüllt wird. Nein, in der Herstellung dieser Produkte wird die gleiche Perfektion erkennbar, die in der Kunstfertigkeit von Haute Couture, Luxuslederwaren und Schmuck steckt. Die gleiche außergewöhnliche Liebe zum Detail motiviert Produktdesigner, Handwerker und Hersteller dazu, Luxusartikel zu kreieren, die für sich selbst sprechen.

Dieses Buch nimmt Sie mit auf die faszinierende Jagd nach
dem perfekten Objekt, auf die kompromisslose Suche
der Designerinnen und Designer nach den besten Formen
und Materialien, um schließlich außergewöhnliche Gegenstände
für den täglichen Gebrauch zu präsentieren, dazu geschaffen,
Jahrzehnte und vielleicht Generationen zu überdauern.
Es ist eine Hommage an herausragende Leistungen und die
außergewöhnlichen Qualitäten, die in ziemlich gewöhnlichen
Objekten verborgen sind. Ich könnte wetten, dass Sie die Seiten
Ihres eigenen Exemplars mit Post-its pflastern (ob deluxe oder
nicht - das spielt keine Rolle!) und sich dabei Ihr tägliches Leben
umgeben von diesen Objekten vorstellen werden.

BRANDS
MARKEN

The brand established in 1987 has gained recognition for Christian Lacroix's Hispanic inspirations manifested through lively colours and theatrical shapes. After the first ready-to-wear collection in 1988 the creations expanded with accessories and perfumes, later followed by jewellery, eyewear, and watches. 2011 marked a turning point for the brand with the launch of Christian Lacroix Maison, focusing on lifestyle products initiated by Sacha Walckhoff (Creative Director since 2010) and Nicolas Topiol (CEO since 2005). This dynamically evolving branch, which actually reinvented the label, includes inspiring Art of Living collections. The upholstery fabrics, wallpapers, cushions, and rugs are striking thanks to their vivid colour palette and lavish patterns, while exquisite tableware delights with sophisticated shapes refined with decorations inspired by the organic world. Numerous collaborations with other brands have enriched the portfolio with notebooks, mobile accessories, and pieces of furniture. The latest addition is a collection of porcelain board games with characteristic romantic, floral motifs.

Die 1987 gegründete Marke erlangte Bekanntheit durch Christian Lacroix´ hispanisch inspirierte Designs mit lebendigen Farben und dramatischen Formen. Nach der ersten Prêt-à-porter-Kollektion 1988 wurde das Angebot um Accessoires und Parfums, später auch um Schmuck, Brillen und Uhren erweitert. Eine Wende in der Firmengeschichte markierte das Jahr 2011 mit der Markteinführung von Christian Lacroix Maison, initiiert von Sacha Walckhoff (Creative Director seit 2009) und Nicolas Topiol (CEO seit 2005), wodurch ein neuer Schwerpunkt auf Lifestyleprodukte gelegt wurde. Durch diesen sich dynamisch entwickelnden Ableger wurde das Label gewissermaßen neu erfunden und umfasst heute kreativ gestaltete Produktlinien zur Verschönerung des alltäglichen Lebens. Die Stoffe, Tapeten, Kissen und Teppiche fallen durch lebendige Farben und üppige Muster auf, und das exquisite Geschirr besticht durch raffinierte Formen und Verzierungen, die Natur und Pflanzenwelt nachempfunden sind. Zahllose Kollaborationen mit anderen Marken erweiterten das Portfolio in der Folge um Notizbücher, Wohnaccessoires und Möbelstücke. Der jüngste Neuzugang ist eine Serie von Porzellan-Gesellschaftsspielen mit typisch romantischen, floralen Motiven.

Before establishing his esteemed fashion house, Christian Dior opened two art galleries – he was an admirer of artists like Picasso, Braque, Matisse, and Dalí – and he worked as an illustrator and designer for other brands. 16 December, 1946, marked the opening of his own couture house. At 30 Avenue Montaigne, which is still the company's Parisian headquarters and now also a gallery space, the designer had a chance to design under his own name for only a decade until his premature death in 1957. In his memoirs, Dior called interior decoration and architecture his first vocation, and today the collection for home, embracing tableware, textiles, objects, and décor, takes a special place in the House's creation as a tribute to refinement and the pleasure of giving. Cultivating the art of living, these objects are decorated with flora and fauna patterns, as well as maps of Paris expressing love for the capital.

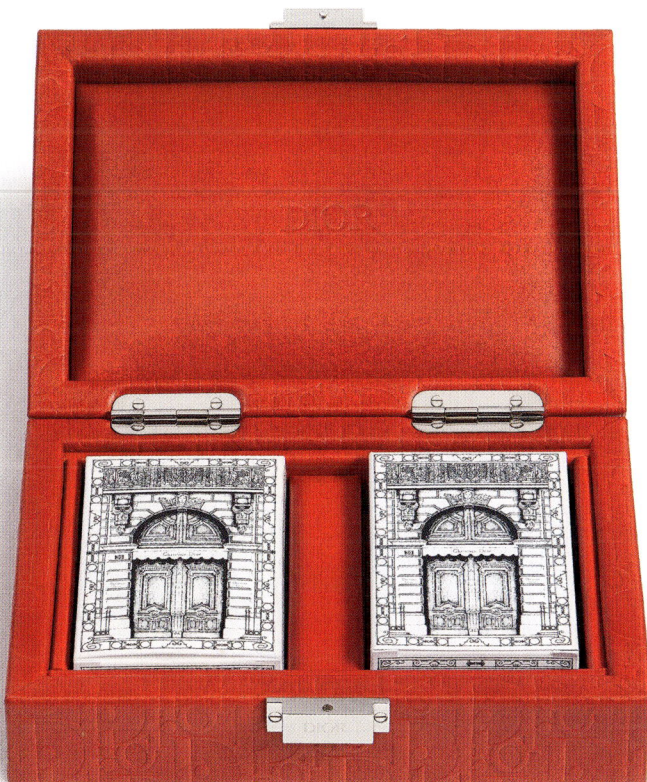

Vor der Gründung seines angesehenen Modehauses eröffnete Christian Dior zwei Kunstgalerien – er war ein Bewunderer von Künstlern wie Picasso, Braque, Matisse und Dalí – und arbeitete als Zeichner und Designer für andere Marken. Am 16. Dezember 1946 eröffnete er sein eigenes Couture-Haus. In der Avenue Montaigne 30, die immer noch der Pariser Hauptsitz des Unternehmens und mittlerweile auch ein Ausstellungsraum ist, fertigte der Designer dann für die Dauer nur eines Jahrzehnts, bis zu seinem frühen Tod im Jahr 1957, unter seinem eigenen Namen Entwürfe an. In seinen Memoiren bezeichnete Dior Inneneinrichtung und Architektur als seine erste Berufung. Heute nimmt die Heimkollektion, die Geschirr, Textilien, Gegenstände und Dekor umfasst, einen besonderen Platz im Hause Dior ein: eine Hommage an die Feinheiten und die Freuden des Schenkens. Verziert sind die Lifestyle-Objekte mit Mustern aus Flora und Fauna sowie mit Stadtplänen von Paris, in denen die Liebe zur Hauptstadt zum Ausdruck kommt.

VERSACE

The eponymous Italian luxury brand was founded in 1978 by Gianni Versace, who fourteen years later* decided to expand the brand's products into accessories, furnishings, and tableware. Since 1997 under the creative direction of Donatella Versace, the Versace Home collection has grown to impressive heights. The range includes bath and bed linens, cushions and blankets, and decorative objects, like vases, candles, and wallpaper, as well as sport and travel accessories, stationery, and even a palette of products for pets. A combination of gold, black and white, Baroque aesthetics, and antique-inspired patterns and motifs, like the iconic Medusa's head, are common threads across the collection. Brilliantly executed masterpieces of Italian artisanship, the designs express an interesting interplay between classical and contemporary. The opulent and elegant objects from the Versace Home collection introduce a hint of luxury into each aspect of everyday life.

* The Versace Home Signature line was created in 1992 (it would later become the Versace Home Collection and then Versace Home).

Die gleichnamige italienische Luxusmarke wurde 1978 von Gianni Versace gegründet, der vierzehn Jahre später* beschloss, die Produkte der Marke um Accessoires, Einrichtungsgegenstände und Geschirr zu erweitern. Seit 1997 wuchs die Versace Home-Kollektion unter der kreativen Leitung von Donatella Versace zu beachtlicher Größe heran. Das Sortiment umfasst Handtücher und Bettlaken, Kissen und Decken, dekorative Objekte wie Vasen, Kerzen und Tapeten sowie Sport- und Reiseaccessoires, Schreibwaren und sogar eine Produktpalette für Haustiere. Die wiederkehrenden Elemente der Kollektion sind Kombinationen aus Gold, Schwarz und Weiß, Barockästhetik und von der Antike inspirierte Muster und Motive, wie der ikonische Medusenkopf. In der meisterhaft ausgeführten italienischen Handwerkskunst zeigt sich ein interessantes Zusammenspiel von Klassik und Moderne. Die opulenten, eleganten Objekte der Versace Home-Kollektion bringen einen Hauch von Luxus in jeden Aspekt des täglichen Lebens.

* Die Linie Versace Home Signature wurde 1992 eingeführt (sie wurde später zur Versace Home Collection und dann zu Versace Home).

Lifestyle accessories from Prada incorporate the brand's distinctive stylistic codes. Celebrating simplicity and pure forms, these objects of everyday use employ a limited colour palette with a classy interplay between black, white, and occasionally red. Inspired by a mix of influences, the wide collection includes objects for the home, like porcelain candles, pillows, and blankets, as well as a wide range of games, sports equipment, and other accessories designed for leisure and outdoor activities. Another component of this powerfully timeless selection are the objects for pets. Some collections include exclusive collector's items, and all have been envisioned to "accompany moments of conviviality, enriching spaces with a unique and refined aesthetic", as the brand's statement reads. Sophisticated yet modern, distinctive yet minimal, these objects become an indispensable addition to everyday life. This book will highlight Prada's world of games, universe for four-legged companions, and last but not least, amazing sports collection.

In die Lifestyle-Accessoires von Prada sind die unverwechselbaren Stilmerkmale der Marke integriert. Die edlen Alltagsgegenstände bestechen durch schlichte, reine Formen und die Verwendung einer limitierten Farbpalette aus Schwarz, Weiß und gelegentlich Rot. Inspiriert von einer Mischung aus Einflüssen umfasst die breite Kollektion Objekte für das Heim, wie Porzellankerzen, Kissen und Decken sowie eine große Auswahl an Spielen, Sportgeräten und anderen Accessoires für Freizeitaktivitäten in der Natur. Ein weiterer Bestandteil dieser ohne Frage zeitlosen Produktpalette sind die Objekte für Haustiere. Einige Kollektionen beinhalten exklusive Sammlerstücke, und alle wurden entworfen, um „Momente der Geselligkeit zu begleiten und Räume mit einer einzigartigen, kultivierten Ästhetik zu bereichern", wie es in der Erklärung der Marke heißt. Ausgereift und doch modern, markant und doch minimalistisch, werden die Objekte schnell unverzichtbar im täglichen Leben. Der Fokus in diesem Buch liegt auf Pradas Spielewelt, den Produkten für vierbeinige Begleiter und nicht zuletzt auf der wunderbaren Sportkollektion.

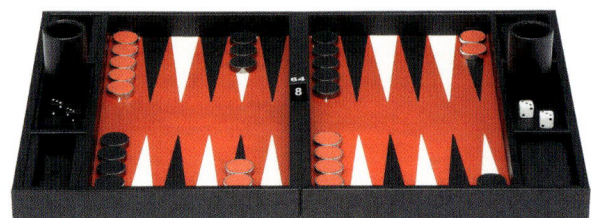

Founded in Rome back in 1925, the couture house FENDI Casa was one of the first to introduce a collection for the home, just like its trend-setting launch of the outdoor line in 2000. Initially produced under a license by the Italian furniture manufacturer Luxury Living, FENDI Casa's programme has evolved into producing creations with sophisticated forms that are inspired by the arches of FENDI Casa headquarters in the Palazzo della Civiltà Italiana and defined by the iconic FF logo or characteristic Pequin stripes. With special attention to detail, the designs celebrate original juxtapositions of materials, woven patterns, reliefs, and meticulous hand stitching. Today, under the creative direction of Silvia Venturini Fendi, the collections are envisioned in collaboration with some of the world's most visionary designers. "In the new FENDI Casa line, beauty finds its purpose in objects with the highest craftsmanship. This is our idea of interior design: elegant and light, classic yet innovative," she remarks.

Gegründet 1925 in Rom, war das Modehaus FENDI Casa eines der ersten mit einer Heimartikelkollektion, die ebenso richtungsweisend war wie im Jahr 2000 der Start der Outdoor-Linie. Ursprünglich unter der Lizenz des italienischen Möbelherstellers Luxury Living produziert, hat sich das Sortiment von FENDI Casa zu Kreationen voll eleganter Formen entwickelt, die von den Bögen des FENDI-Hauptsitzes im Palazzo della Civiltà Italiana inspiriert sind und durch das ikonische FF-Logo oder die typischen Pequin-Streifen definiert werden. Den Entwürfen sieht man die besondere Liebe zum Detail an; originelle Materialkombinationen, gewebte Muster, Reliefs und akkurate Handstickerei. Heute werden die Kollektionen unter der kreativen Leitung von Silvia Venturini Fendi in Zusammenarbeit mit einigen der innovativsten Designerinnen und Designern der Welt entworfen. „In den Objekten der neuen FENDI-Casa-Linie wird Schönheit durch höchste Handwerkskunst zum Ausdruck gebracht. Das ist unsere Vorstellung von Interior Design: elegant und leicht, klassisch und dennoch innovativ", so Venturini Fendi.

The French luxury fashion house specialising in leather goods was founded in 1854. The Objets Nomades Collection was initiated in 2012 to engage celebrated designers from around the world in an inspiring dialogue between their styles, the essence of the legendary brand, and leather as traditional material.
The accessories, furniture, and lighting design have travel as a leading motif. The goal is to envision experimental yet functional pieces at the intersection of designers' artistic visions and Louis Vuitton artisans' craftsmanship. From a foldable stool to a hammock, from a vase to a lamp, a wide range of limited-edition objects pushes the limits of the material, demonstrating the possibilities, often unexpected, of working with leather. Vivid colours, fanciful shapes, and varied textures create a sophisticated, and continuously expanding, collection of novel travel objects. The project also pays homage to Louis Vuitton's historical special orders, like the iconic Bed Trunk produced in 1874 for French explorer Pierre Savorgnan de Brazza.

Das französische, auf Lederwaren spezialisierte Luxusmodehaus wurde 1854 gegründet. 2012 wurde die Objets Nomades Collection ins Leben gerufen, um berühmte Designerinnen und Designer aus der ganzen Welt in einen inspirierenden Dialog zwischen ihren Stilen, dem Markenkern der legendären Firma und Leder als traditionellem Material treten zu lassen. Inspiriert sind die Designs der Accessoires, Möbel und Lampen vom Reisen. Das Ziel ist die Kreation experimenteller und dennoch funktionaler Stücke, die die künstlerischen Visionen der Kreativen und die traditionelle Handwerkskunst von Louis Vuitton miteinander verbinden. Vom faltbaren Hocker bis zur Hängematte, von der Vase bis zur Lampe – eine breite Palette limitiert aufgelegter Objekte lotet die Grenzen des Materials aus und demonstriert die oft unerwarteten Möglichkeiten des Werkstoffs Leder. Kräftige Farben, phantasievolle Formen und unterschiedliche Beschaffenheiten ergeben eine anspruchsvolle und ständig wachsende Kollektion neuartiger Reiseartikel. Das Projekt ist auch eine Hommage an Louis Vuittons historische Sonderanfertigungen, wie den legendären Bed Trunk, der 1874 für den französischen Entdecker Pierre Savorgnan de Brazza angefertigt wurde.

Young Guccio Gucci, inspired by his work as a porter in the London Savoy hotel in 1987, had the bold dream of wanting luggage to bear his name, and eventually became a world-renowned icon of Italian craft. Since 1921 when Gucci opened his first boutique in his native Florence, the company has celebrated Italian artisanal excellence. With the goal of redefining luxury, the house regularly grows the collections from ready-to-wear, shoes, and leather goods to bags, jewellery, and watches. The decades of the 1970s and 1980s already saw the rise of lifestyle objects starting with board games, tennis gear, dog carriers, and décor. Today this branch also includes stationery, travel sets, tableware, furniture, textiles, sporting goods, and the Gucci Pet Collection, which offers a wide selection of accessories for four-legged friends. The high-quality pieces are defined by characteristic Gucci symbols and prints, as well as a distinctive colour palette and great attention to detail.

Der junge Guccio Gucci, der 1897 als Portier im Londoner Savoy Hotel arbeitete, hatte, inspiriert von dieser Erfahrung, den kühnen Traum von Gepäckstücken, die seinen Namen tragen sollten, und tatsächlich wurde er schließlich zu einer weltberühmten Ikone italienischer Handwerkskunst. Seit 1921, als Gucci die erste Boutique in seiner Heimatstadt Florenz eröffnete, steht das Unternehmen für außerordentliches italienisches Design. Mit dem Ziel, Luxus neu zu definieren, erweitert das Haus regelmäßig seine Kollektionen von Konfektionskleidung, Schuhen und Lederwaren bis hin zu Taschen, Schmuck und Uhren. Bereits in den 1970er und 1980er Jahren entstanden mit Brettspielen, Tennisausrüstung, Tragetaschen für Hunde und Dekorationsartikeln die ersten Lifestyle-Objekte. Heute umfasst dieser Zweig des Unternehmens auch Schreibwaren, Reisesets, Geschirr, Möbel, Textilien, Sportartikel und die Gucci Pet Collection, die eine große Auswahl an Accessoires für die vierbeinigen Freunde bereithält. Die hochwertigen Stücke zeichnen sich durch die charakteristischen Gucci-Symbole und -Drucke sowie eine unverwechselbare Farbpalette und viel Liebe zum Detail aus.

In 1997, after 44 years, the founders
of the brand, Rosita and Ottavio Missoni,
decided to pass the fashion creation on
to the next generation and focus exclusively
on collections for the home. In November
2000 the Missoni Home collection was
officially presented in New York, starting
the successful development of the new facet
of the brand that has since been awarded
multiple times internationally. Bath linens,
cushions and throws, poufs, and art de la table
create a rich offering of the new branch of
the legendary Italian brand, additionally
enriched by numerous collaborations with
leading design manufacturers, like Roche
Bobois. The omnipresent spirit of Missoni
is expressed through their signature zigzag
motif in countless variants, on textiles to wear
as well as furnishings to decorate interiors. In
each case, the dynamic pattern is enhanced
by an equally vibrant composition of colours
that turn even a simple object into a powerful
element of any interior space.

1997 entschieden sich die Markenbegründer,
Rosita und Ottavio Missoni, nach 44 Jahren
im Geschäft die Leitung der Modelinie
an die nachfolgende Generation zu übergeben
und sich ausschließlich auf Kollektionen
für den Wohnbereich zu konzentrieren.
Im November 2000 wurde die Missoni Home
collection offiziell in New York präsentiert,
womit der erfolgreiche Startschuss für die
neue Ausrichtung der Marke fiel, die seitdem
mehrfach international ausgezeichnet
wurde. Bademäntel, Kissen und Handtücher,
Polsterhocker und Tafelgeschirr bilden das
umfangreiche Angebot des neuen Ablegers
des legendären italienischen Labels,
das zusätzlich durch zahlreiche Kooperationen
mit führenden Unternehmen der Sparte,
wie etwa Roche Bobois, bereichert wird.
Für den Wiedererkennungswert von Missoni
sorgt das unverkennbare Zickzackmuster,
das in allen denkbaren Variationen daher-
kommt; sowohl auf Kleidern als auch auf
Einrichtungsgegenständen. Zusätzlich wird
das dynamische Muster durch eine ebenso
lebendige Farbkomposition hervorgehoben,
was auch das schlichteste Accessoire in
ein kraftvolles Statement verwandelt.

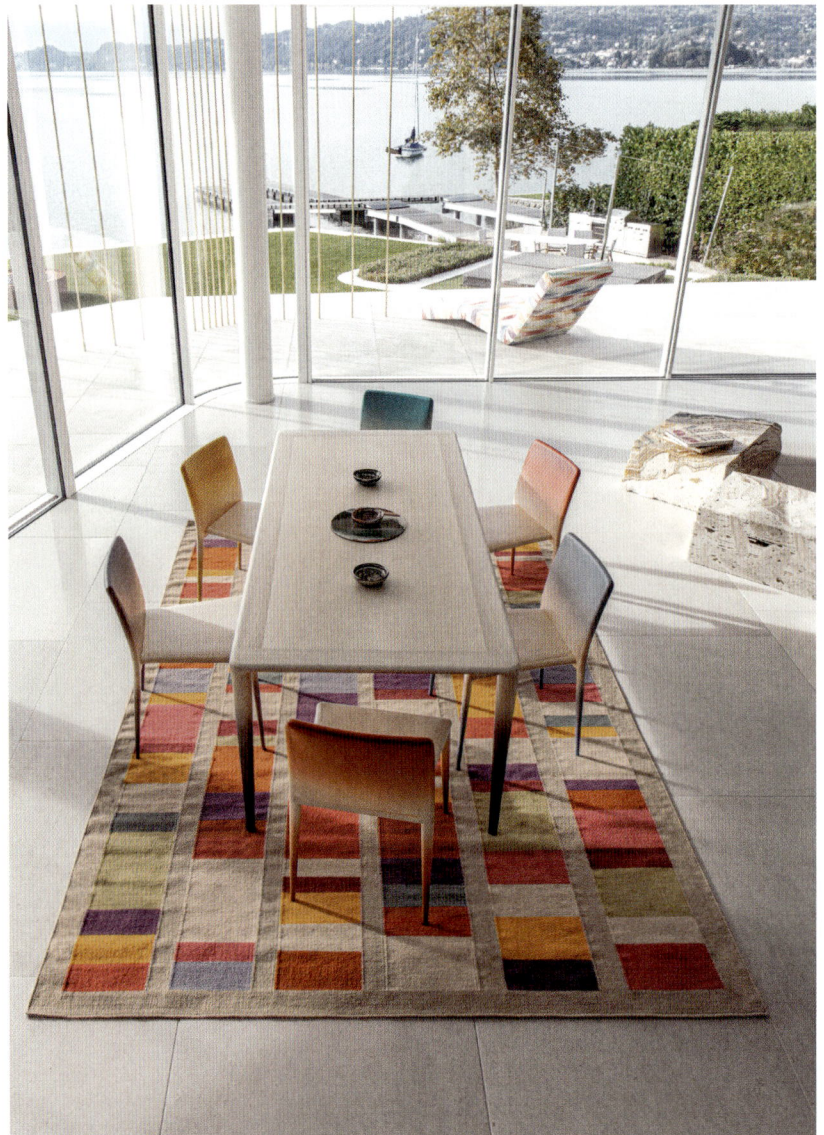

Since 1985 Domenico Dolce & Stefano Gabbana have created a distinctive universe of fashion and accessories famous for fantasy animal prints, detailed embroidery, the exquisite use of lace or Italian staples, and vibrant floral patterns. This unique aesthetic is at the essence of the Dolce & Gabbana collection for the home. After the first successful collaborations on homewares including limited-edition hand-painted fridges and small kitchen appliances for Smeg adorned with iconic patterns, the duo decided to launch the first, and highly ambitious, home collection in 2022. The products, ranging from seating and dining furniture to decorative objects, to tableware and home linens, are available in four iconic motifs reflecting various lifestyles: Mediterranean Blue, Sicilian Carretto, Leopard, and Zebra. Infusing interiors with joy and chicness, the lavishly decorated objects were crafted in collaboration with traditional Italian brands and artisans, including blown glass objects made in Murano, ceramics hand-painted in Sicily, and fabrics produced in Como.

Seit der Gründung 1985 ist das unverwechselbare Mode- und Accessoires-Universum von Domenico Dolce & Stefano Gabbana berühmt für fantasievolle Tierdrucke, detaillierte Stickereien, die raffinierte Verwendung von Spitze, klassische italienische Motive und prächtige florale Muster. Diese einzigartige Ästhetik ist ebenfalls die Grundlage für die Dolce & Gabbana Casa-Kollektion. Denn nach den ersten erfolgreichen Kooperationen für Haushaltswaren, darunter handbemalte Kühlschränke in limitierter Auflage und kleine Küchengeräte für Smeg mit ikonischen Mustern, brachte das Duo 2022 die erste und sehr ehrgeizige Heimkollektion auf den Markt. Die Produkte, die von Wohn- und Esszimmermöbeln über Dekoelemente bis hin zu Geschirr, Kissen und Decken reichen, sind in vier Kultmotiven für verschiedene Wohnstile erhältlich: Mediterranean Blue, Sicilian Carretto, Leopard und Zebra. Die aufwendig dekorierten Gegenstände strahlen pure Lebensfreude aus und werten jeden Innenraum auf. Hergestellt wurden sie in Zusammenarbeit mit italienischen Traditionsmarken und Kunsthandwerkern, unter anderem finden sich mundgeblasene Gläser aus Murano, handbemalte Keramik aus Sizilien und Stoffe aus Como.

Baccarat's long history started in 1764, when it was established by a group of craftsmen. Over the decades, they have perfected their secret formula for obtaining the purest crystal in the world. Starting in 1855 with the first World Fair in Paris, Baccarat gained international recognition that was followed by orders from royalty and the world's most powerful figures, like the Emperor of Japan, Maharajas, Tsar Nicholas II, and Napoleon III. Baccarat's dazzling creations have made the brand the legend of crystal, which it remains today. Thanks to a team of in-house researchers, their ancestral techniques have evolved over the decades to push the boundaries of this sophisticated art. With a strong sense of being in tune with the times, Baccarat's luxury objects are envisioned as works of art and crafted to bring luminous joy and pleasure to everyday life. The craftsmanship with its centuries-long traditions demonstrates an extraordinary heritage which the contemporary creations draw from.

Die lange Geschichte von Baccarat begann 1764, als die Firma von einer Gruppe von Glasarbeitern gegründet wurde. Im Laufe der Jahrzehnte hat das Unternehmen seine geheime Technik für das reinste Kristall der Welt perfektioniert. 1855, bei der ersten Weltausstellung in Paris, erlangte Baccarat zum ersten Mal internationale Anerkennung, was in der Folge zu Aufträgen von Königen und den mächtigsten Persönlichkeiten ihrer Zeit führte, darunter der Kaiser von Japan, Maharadschas, Zar Nikolaus II. und Napoleon III. Die schillernden Kreationen von Baccarat haben die Marke in der Welt des Kristalls zur Legende gemacht, die sie bis heute geblieben ist. Dank eines Teams von internen Wissenschaftlerinnen und Wissenschaftlern haben sich die angestammten Techniken im Laufe der Jahrzehnte weiterentwickelt, und damit die Grenzen dieser anspruchsvollen Kunst erweitert. Mit einem starken Gespür für den Zeitgeist werden die Luxusobjekte von Baccarat als Kunstwerke betrachtet und hergestellt, um funkelnde Freude und reinstes Vergnügen in den Alltag zu bringen. Die Kristallkunst verfügt durch ihre jahrhundertealten Traditionen über ein außergewöhnliches Erbe, aus dem die zeitgenössischen Kreationen Inspiration schöpfen.

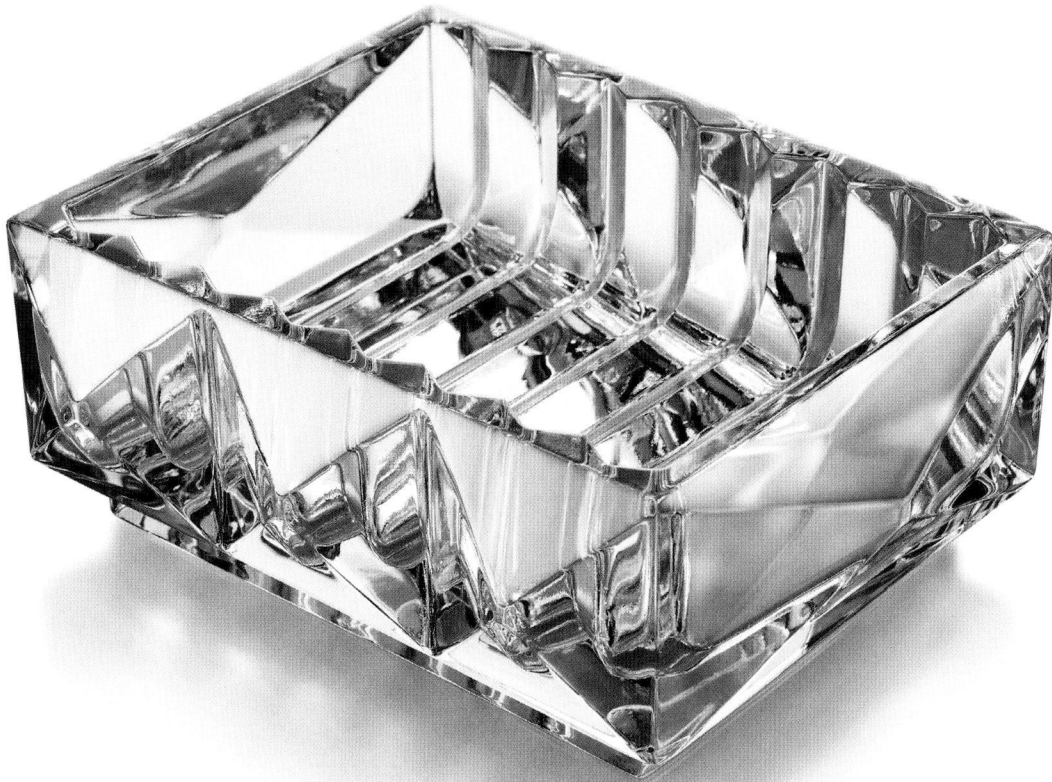

With its key statement – our dogs are our modern day horses – PAGERIE was founded as a luxury fashion house for pets. With a focus on the highest quality and timeless elegance, as well as functionality, the brand offers exquisite collections of accessories, for dogs and their owners. These exceptional pieces, which are still somehow striking in their simplicity, fill a gap of fashion-forward accessories and sophisticated embellishments for pets. "Reminiscent of a time that valued heirloom-quality items that stood the test of time, we strive to continue the legacy of centuries-old heritage and precision craftsmanship through quality, sustainability and design", the brand states. The finest materials are consciously sourced with sustainability in mind and are based on extensive research, while the manufacturing processes are planned to minimise waste and environmental impact, like the choice of real, vegetable-tanned leather that is biodegradable and reduces the output of toxic chemicals. Durable, classy, and practical, accessories from PAGERIE embody quiet luxury for man's best friends.

Ganz im Sinne der Unternehmensphilosophie – unsere Hunde sind die Pferde der heutigen Zeit – wurde Pagerie als Luxusmodehaus für Haustiere gegründet. Der Fokus liegt auf höchster Qualität, zeitloser Eleganz und Funktionalität, und die Marke bietet exquisite Kollektionen von Accessoires, für Hunde und ihre Besitzer. Diese außergewöhnlichen Stücke, die trotz ihrer Schlichtheit ins Auge fallen, schließen eine Lücke im Bereich modischer Accessoires und anspruchsvoller Ausstattung für Haustiere. „In Erinnerung an eine Zeit, in der hochwertige Gegenstände von langer Lebensdauer geschätzt wurden, setzen wir, durch Qualität, Nachhaltigkeit und Design, das jahrhundertealte Erbe außergewöhnlicher Handwerkskunst fort", so das Unternehmen. Die edelsten Materialien werden bewusst und basierend auf umfangreicher Forschung im Hinblick auf Nachhaltigkeit ausgewählt, zugleich werden bei der Herstellung Abfall und Umweltbelastung minimiert, beispielsweise durch die Wahl von echtem, pflanzlich gegerbtem Leder, das biologisch abbaubar ist und den Ausstoß giftiger Chemikalien auf ein Minimum reduziert. Langlebig, edel und praktisch – Accessoires von PAGERIE verkörpern zurückhaltenden Luxus für die besten Freunde des Menschen.

COLLABORATIONS

KOLLABORATIONEN

Cristina Celestino x FENDI Casa

You have designed quite a few projects for FENDI Casa. Could you tell us how this fruitful collaboration started?

The collaboration with FENDI Casa was initiated in 2016 at Art Basel Miami upon the invitation of Maria Cristina Didero, the curator of the exhibition that year. We conceptualised a collection named "The Happy Room", which comprises furnishings for the VIP Room, embodying an elegant and sophisticated spatial concept, designed for replication by the Maison within its boutiques globally. It represents a sanctuary of intimacy and excellence, offering a private and personal experience. The space enhances the value of time spent in self-reflection, where the notion of time is embraced as an inherent design virtue of each meticulously crafted piece, recognising the time invested in producing finely detailed objects.

Hence, from this collaboration, the partnership with FENDI and Silvia Venturini Fendi emerged. In 2019, she reached out to me to design a collection and set up an exhibition for FENDI and FENDI Casa. The title was "Back Home", and it aimed to commemorate a return to the origins of the FENDICasa brand, celebrating the strong connection with the Roman Maison.

What is the starting point of each design – is there a kind of brief or theme to follow or do you receive carte blanche? .

When we receive carte blanche we always start with in-depth research: this entails delving into the brand's distinctive stylistic language and collaborating closely with their archival materials. This approach allows us to draw inspiration from the brand's heritage while infusing our designs with a contemporary and innovative touch, imbued with an international aura, while simultaneously paying meticulous attention to a higher level of craftsmanship and quality.

The shape of an arch at the Palazzo della Civiltà, home to FENDI, was an inspiration for the chair designed in 2023. Where do you draw your inspiration for other designs and collections?

As I said, we always look back to history to search for inspiration. The arch stands as a quintessentially Roman innovation, akin to the legacy of FENDI's architectural identity. Its presence is ubiquitous, gracing ancient structures like the Colosseum and the Basilica of Maxentius, to the more contemporary Palazzo della Civiltà in the EUR district in Rome—now serving as the Maison's headquarters. Commemorating this architectural motif through a chair, an everyday object, felt not just appropriate but imperative to me.

In the 'Back Home' collection you interpret FENDI's iconic Pequin striped motif – is it difficult to find a good balance between one's style and the Maison's identity?

I am naturally drawn to geometries, whether found in nature or works created by humans. It was instinctive for me, therefore, to employ that element to tell a new story, placing it in a fresh and different context. We explored the realm of scale, employing distinct colours and experimenting with various materials to offer a contemporary interpretation of the Pequin traditional motif.

I find 'The Happy Room' collection particularly complex with a great combination of materials and textures. What does the creative process look like when you envision the whole collection?

The designs exhibit harmonious and rounded forms, with each piece – from tables to chairs, screens to mirrors, lamps to dressing tables – capturing attention through a distinctive emphasis on materials, colours, and expert craftsmanship. The project's leitmotif revolves around inlaid materials, a hallmark of the Maison's style. This is evident in the graphic approach, where contrasting marble and onyx are artfully employed for the table tops, and in the mesmerising interplay of reflective, coloured antique-finish segments on both the mirror and the screen. The entire composition appears cohesive, yet, on an identity level, it is also intricate: the objects can also speak for themselves.

Which project was most challenging for you? And is there anything you would dream of designing for the world of FENDI Casa?

When I think back, I always think fondly of the first project. The first times are always very exciting and full of new challenges. Our collaboration continues, so every year there is new furniture to be designed, to fill people's homes with beauty, and I would love to design a new sofa!

You work with various brands. Do you see differences between design brands and couture houses in terms of thinking about objects for everyday use?

Collaborating with fashion houses on themes related to living brings about different reflections: there is, in any case, an emphasis on craftsmanship and a departure from mass production. Often fashion houses maintain extensive historical archives, providing a wealth of material from which to draw inspiration. There is a more open culture towards experimental forms and, perhaps, greater freedom. Fewer constraints mean more possibilities to explore a full spectrum of creative avenues!

Sie haben einige Projekte für FENDI Casa designt. Können Sie uns verraten, wie diese fruchtbare Zusammenarbeit begonnen hat?

Die Zusammenarbeit mit FENDI Casa kam 2016 auf der Art Basel Miami zustande, auf Einladung von Maria Cristina Didero, der Kuratorin der Ausstellung in jenem Jahr. Wir entwarfen eine Kollektion mit dem Namen „The Happy Room", die aus Möbeln für einen VIP-Bereich bestand und über ein ausgeklügeltes, elegantes Raumkonzept verfügte, das von der Maison in ihren Boutiquen auf der ganzen Welt nachgebaut werden konnte. Der so konzipierte Bereich wird zu einem exklusiven Refugium der Ruhe und verhilft zu einer sehr intimen, persönlichen Erfahrung. Der Raum unterstreicht den Wert der Zeit, die man mit Selbstreflexion verbringt. Die Zeit selbst wohnt als besondere Eigenschaft jedem akribisch gefertigten Stück inne, und der zeitliche Aufwand, der in der Herstellung detailliert gearbeiteter Objekte steckt, wird gebührend gewürdigt.

Aus dieser Kollaboration entstand also die Partnerschaft mit FENDI und Silvia Venturini Fendi. 2019 nahm sie Kontakt zu mir auf, damit ich eine Kollektion samt Ausstellung für FENDI und FENDI Casa entwarf. Der Titel lautete „Back Home", womit an die Ursprünge der Marke FENDI Casa angeknüpft und die enge Verbindung zum römischen Mutterkonzern zelebriert werden sollte.

Wie fangen Sie Ihre Designs an – gibt es Vorgaben oder Themen, denen Sie folgen müssen, oder lässt man Ihnen vollkommen freie Hand?

Es kommt drauf an, aber wenn es keine Vorgaben gibt, beginnen wir immer mit einer eingehenden Recherche: Dazu gehört, dass wir uns mit der unverwechselbaren Formensprache der Marke und den in der Vergangenheit verwendeten Materialien auseinandersetzen. Mit diesem Ansatz können wir uns vom Erbe der Marke inspirieren lassen und den neuen Entwürfen einen zeitgenössischen, innovativen, internationaleren Touch verleihen, während wir gleichzeitig auf ein hohes Niveau an Handwerkskunst und Qualität achten.

Die Inspiration für den 2023 designten Stuhl kam von der Bogenform des Palazzo della Civiltà, dem Hauptsitz von FENDI. Woher nehmen Sie die Inspiration für andere Designs und Kollektionen?

Wie gesagt, wir suchen unsere Inspiration immer in der Geschichte der Marke. Der Bogen ist eine typisch römische Besonderheit und steht gewissermaßen für das architektonische Erbe von FENDIs Identität. Er ist allgegenwärtig und ziert antike Bauwerke wie das Kolosseum und die Maxentiusbasilika ebenso wie den zeitgenössischen Palazzo della Civiltà im EUR-Viertel in Rom, der heute als Hauptsitz der Maison dient. Diesem architektonischen Motiv mit einem Alltagsgegenstand, einem Stuhl, zu gedenken, erschien mir nicht nur angemessen, sondern sogar notwendig.

In der Kollektion „Back Home" interpretieren Sie FENDIs ikonische Pequin-Streifen neu – ist es schwierig, eine gute Balance zwischen dem eigenen Stil und der Markenidentität zu finden?

Mich zieht es automatisch zu geometrischen Formen, sei es in der Natur oder in von Menschen gemachten Werken. Insofern habe ich ganz instinktiv mit diesem Element gearbeitet, es in einen anderen, unverbrauchten Kontext gesetzt, um eine neue Geschichte zu erzählen. Für die zeitgemäße Interpretation des traditionellen Pequin-Motivs haben wir mit dessen Größenverhältnissen und verschiedenen Materialien experimentiert und mit einem klaren Farbkonzept gearbeitet.

Die Kollektion „Happy Room" scheint mir besonders komplex zu sein, Sie verwenden dort sehr verschiedene Materialien mit unterschiedlicher Beschaffenheit. Wie sieht der kreative Prozess aus, wenn Sie sich eine Kollektion als Ganzes ausmalen?

Die Entwürfe zeichnen sich durch harmonische und abgerundete Formen aus. Jedes Stück – vom Tisch bis zum Stuhl, vom Paravent bis zum Spiegel, von der Lampe bis zur Frisierkommode – besticht durch die besondere Betonung des Materials, die Farbgebung und die meisterhafte Fertigung. Das Leitmotiv dieses Projekts sind die Intarsien, die ein Markenzeichen des Hauses sind. Die grafischen Elemente machen das deutlich; die kontrastierenden Marmor- und Onyxplatten, die kunstvoll in die Tischplatten eingelassen sind, und das hypnotische Zusammenspiel von reflektierenden und farbigen Segmenten mit antikem Finish auf Spiegel und Paravent. Die Gesamtkomposition wirkt kohärent, enthält aber gleichzeitig noch eine weitere Ebene: Die Objekte haben auch für sich selbst betrachtet eine besondere Wirkung.

Welches Projekt hat Sie am meisten herausgefordert? Und gibt es etwas, dass Sie unbedingt für FENDI Casa designen wollen würden?

Rückblickend denke ich immer gern an das erste Projekt zurück. Das erste Mal ist immer besonders aufregend und voller neuer Herausforderungen. Unsere Zusammenarbeit wird fortgesetzt, ich entwerfe also jedes Jahr neue Möbel, um die Häuser der Menschen mit schönen Dingen zu füllen, und sehr gern würde ich ein neues Sofa kreieren!

Sie arbeiten mit verschiedenen Unternehmen zusammen. Erkennen Sie einen Unterschied zwischen Designermarken und Modehäusern beim Entwerfen von Alltagsgegenständen?

Die Zusammenarbeit mit Modehäusern führt beim Thema Wohnen zu anderen Überlegungen: Auf jeden Fall liegt der Schwerpunkt auf der Handwerkskunst und der Abkehr von der Massenproduktion. Oft unterhalten Modehäuser umfangreiche historische Archive, die eine Fülle von Material zur Inspiration bieten. Es herrscht eine offenere Kultur gegenüber experimentellen Formen und vielleicht auch eine größere Freiheit. Weniger Zwänge bedeuten mehr Möglichkeiten, kreative Wege auszuloten!

Sacha Walckhoff x Christian Lacroix Maison

You became the brand's Creative Director in 2010 and it was your idea to expand the brand towards lifestyle design and home decor – what was this shift driven by?
I'd say it was motivated by necessity, instinct, a certain vision of what Christian Lacroix could become, and a fair degree of recklessness!

The company was going through difficult times. It had been sold to the Falic Group by LVMH in 2005, as the latter wanted to get rid of the company, the only one within the group that they had founded, and that never operated profitably. The House Christian Lacroix, established in 1987, was losing money year after year. No one believed in the brand any more, and Christian Lacroix himself had thrown in the towel in July 2009, when he stopped coming to the studio …

We urgently needed to reinvent ourselves. The Haute Couture and ready-to-wear collections were in the red and were set aside to invest only in the men's and accessories collections, which were still profitable at the time, but not enough to keep the company afloat. It was vital to find new opportunities that would be consistent with the spirit and history of this unique company. That's when Nicolas Topiol, who has been CEO since 2005, and I decided to explore the world of lifestyle. From the very first contacts we made, we sensed that this idea was met with genuine interest by the main players in this industry, which was totally unknown to us at the time, and we embarked on the adventure.

What was the most challenging and most fascinating in creating a completely new branch of luxury couture brand? How would you describe your initial goals?
After the company's insolvency, announced in 2009, we had quite a difficult time. All French media were against us. Christian Lacroix portrayed himself as the victim of an American investor, which was far from the truth, and it made our task even harder. The first sign of hope came from the home decoration and design key people, who welcomed us with open arms and immediately understood the potential of a brand with such a powerful creative heritage and international reputation. Our primary goals at the time were to survive and evolve into a creative and profitable company so that we could pay off our debts, which, by 2010, were astronomical. Taking on a major challenge like this is always exciting, and we were very lucky to meet Tricia Guild from Designers Guild. In partnership with her, we laid the foundations of

the lifestyle collection, which quickly found its audience. .

Are your mixed French, Swiss, Slavic, and African roots a heritage that you draw from? What is your biggest source of inspiration?
There's naturally a little bit of myself in the collections, but the truth is that the eclecticism of my origins has helped me to embrace the values of diversity and openness that constitute this house's DNA.

I'm particularly interested in the words used to describe it, which are more stimulating than our history, however rich and flamboyant it may be: Polychromy, contrast, joie de vivre, historicism … the list is very long, very meaningful, and leaves me completely free to create new motifs. Some of styles that have contributed to our current success have never been featured in the collections preserved in our archives. And yet our audience identifies them with the Lacroix style.

What is your favourite collection so far and why?
It's always the next one of course!

On a more serious note, "Butterfly parade", the best selling of all our collections since 2012, is still a very important design of mine because it's the one that gave me the keys to my creative freedom.

It depicts a flight of butterflies which, if you look closely, is composed not only of butterflies but also of abstract motifs that may evoke a form of beetle. It's a very successful print that is both classic and innovative, and has been copied and re-copied many times. It has been the source of the "butterfly" trend, which has switched from decoration to fashion in recent years.

Gabrielle Chanel herself said that true success was being copied!
However, it was the comment made by a journalist at the press launch of this design that left a lasting impression on me. She congratulated me on bringing this design from the Christian Lacroix archives back to life, because she felt it was perfectly symbolic of the lightness and joie de vivre that Christian Lacroix meant to everyone. I thanked her, but of course didn't tell her that there had never been any butterfly prints in the Lacroix collections before 2012! Thanks to her I understood something important: Provided I designed prints that echoed the audience's perception of Lacroix, I was free to invent whatever I wanted. That day, I was handed the keys to my creative freedom.

Galison for stationery, Designers Guild for fabrics and wallpapers, Vista Alegre for porcelain, Roche Bobois for furnitures and Schmidt for kitchens – what are the factors for starting a collaboration with a new brand?

That's where instinct comes in, just like when you decide to get into a relationship! I have all sorts of criteria that determine whether or not I can envisage a new partnership. One of the most important is of course to feel the desire, on both sides, to invent something new and unprecedented.

You work on a large scope of objects – from smartphone accessories to bathroom equipment and wallpaper, to name but a few. Can you please tell us more about the creative process and how you translate the spirit of Christian Lacroix into various designs?

I am lucky enough to work for a brand where fantasy, lightness, and boldness are very appealing and resonate with a wide audience. We have quite a few offers of all kinds and we make a point of considering them all. Then, if a product, even an unexpected one, catches our attention, we look together to see how it can be added to our collections. Our unique eclecticism is the main reason why we are able to deal with so many different partners. It is also what strengthens our notoriety, and makes us popular across the generations.

What is your biggest dream for the brand's lifestyle collections in the future?

Christian Lacroix Maison has been in operation for 13 years. Our present only exists thanks to our past. We have taken over, albeit in a different way, from a great story that began more than 35 years ago. I hope that this brand will live on for a long time to come. As for the future of the Christian Lacroix lifestyle collections, I prefer to be surprised by an unexpected proposal, like the interior design project for a luxury building in Guatemala that we've just been working on. Life is full of surprises – you just have to trust it.

Sie wurden 2010 Creative Director des Unternehmens und es war Ihre Idee, die Marke in Richtung Lifestyle-Design und Wohnkultur zu erweitern. Was war der Grund für diesen Wandel?
Ich würde sagen, es war eine Mischung aus Notwendigkeit, Instinkt, einer gewissen Vision von dem, was Christian Lacroix werden könnte, und einer gehörigen Portion Leichtsinn!

Das Unternehmen machte gerade eine schwierige Phase durch. Es war 2005 von LVMH an Falic verkauft worden, weil es das einzige innerhalb der Konzerngruppe war, das nie Profit abgeworfen hatte. Das 1987 gegründete Haus Christian Lacroix kostete Jahr für Jahr Geld. Niemand glaubte mehr an die Marke, und Christian Lacroix selbst hatte im Juli 2009 das Handtuch geworfen, da kam er nicht mehr ins Studio …

Wir mussten uns dringend neu erfinden. Sowohl die Haute Couture- als auch die Prêt-à-porter-Kollektion schrieben rote Zahlen und wurden zurückgestellt, um den Fokus auf die Herren- und die Accessoire-Kollektion zu legen, die zu diesem Zeitpunkt zwar noch rentabel waren, allerdings nicht ausreichten, um das Unternehmen langfristig über Wasser zu halten. Es mussten unbedingt neue Möglichkeiten her, die überdies mit dem Geist und der Geschichte dieses einzigartigen Unternehmens in Einklang standen. Das war der Moment, als Nicolas Topiol, der seit 2005 CEO ist, und ich beschlossen, die Welt des Wohnens zu erkunden. Schon bei den ersten Kontakten, die wir knüpften, spürten wir, dass diese Idee bei den führenden Köpfen dieser uns bis dahin völlig unbekannten Branche auf echtes Interesse stieß, und so ließen wir uns auf das Abenteuer ein.

Was war die größte Herausforderung dabei, einen völlig neuen Ableger einer Luxusmodekette zu erschaffen? Was hat Sie am meisten daran begeistert? Welche Ziele hatten Sie sich zu Anfang gesteckt?
Nach der Insolvenz des Unternehmens 2009 hatten wir es schwer. Die französischen Medien waren gegen uns. Christian Lacroix stellte sich selbst als Opfer eines amerikanischen Investors dar, was von der Wahrheit weit entfernt war, und das machte es nur noch schlimmer. Der erste Hoffnungsschimmer kam von den Schlüsselpersonen aus dem Lifestylesektor, die uns mit offenen Armen empfingen und sofort begriffen, welches Potential in einer Marke steckt, die ein so herausragendes kreatives Erbe in sich trägt und weltweit Anerkennung genießt. Unser vornehmliches Ziel zu jener Zeit war es, zu überleben und uns zu einer kreativen und zugleich profitablen Firma zu entwickeln, damit wir die Schulden begleichen konnten, die damals, 2010, astronomisch hoch waren. Eine so große Herausforderung wie diese anzunehmen, ist immer aufregend, und wir hatten großes Glück, Tricia Guild von Designers Guild kennenzulernen.

In Kooperation mit ihr legten wir den Grundstein für die Einrichtungssparte, die dann schnell ihre Anhänger fand.

Ziehen Sie Inspiration aus Ihren französischen, schweizerischen, slawischen und afrikanischen Wurzeln? Was beeinflusst Ihre Arbeit am stärksten?
Natürlich steckt auch ein wenig von mir selbst in den Kollektionen, doch eigentlich schätze ich gerade aufgrund meiner Herkunft die Vielfalt und Offenheit, die dieses Modehaus im Kern ausmachen.

Mich interessieren vor allem die Worte, mit denen es beschrieben wird, die anregender sind als die Geschichte, so bunt und vielschichtig sie auch sein mag: Polychromie, Kontrast, Joie de vivre, Historismus … die Liste ist sehr lang, sehr aussagekräftig und lässt mir völlige Freiheit, neue Motive zu kreieren. Einige der Stile, die zu unserem heutigen Erfolg beigetragen haben, waren in den Archiven noch nicht vertreten. Und doch werden sie von der Kundschaft eindeutig mit dem Lacroix-Stil assoziiert.

Welche ist bisher Ihre Lieblingskollektion, und warum?
Das ist natürlich immer die, die als nächstes kommt!

Spaß beiseite, „Butterfly parade", unsere bestverkaufte Kollektion seit 2012, gehört immer noch zu meinen wichtigsten Designs, denn dort fand ich den Schlüssel zu meiner kreativen Freiheit.

Zu sehen ist ein Schwarm Schmetterlinge, der bei näherer Betrachtung nicht nur aus Schmetterlingen besteht, sondern auch aus abstrakten Motiven, die an Insekten erinnern. Es ist ein überaus erfolgreiches Design, sowohl klassisch als auch innovativ, das mittlerweile oft kopiert wurde. Tatsächlich begründet es den Schmetterling-Trend, der in den letzten Jahren von der Inneneinrichtung auf die Mode übergeschwappt ist.

Gabrielle Chanel höchstpersönlich sagte einmal, dass wahrer Erfolg darin besteht, kopiert zu werden!

Wie dem auch sei, bleibenden Eindruck hat bei mir vor allem der Kommentar einer Journalistin bei der Pressekonferenz gemacht, als wir den Entwurf präsentierten. Sie gratulierte mir dazu, dass ich eines der alten Christian-Lacroix-Designs wieder zum Leben erweckt hatte, denn für sie entsprach es vollkommen der Leichtigkeit und Lebensfreude, die Christian Lacroix für alle verkörpert. Ich dankte ihr, erzählte ihr aber natürlich nicht, dass es vor 2012 nie irgendwelche Schmetterlinge in den Lacroix-Kollektionen gegeben hatte. Durch diese Begegnung wurde mir etwas Wichtiges klar: Solange ich Entwürfe kreierte, die dem entsprachen, was gemeinhin von Lacroix erwartet wurde, konnte ich erfinden, was immer ich wollte. An jenem Tag bekam ich den Schlüssel zu meiner künstlerischen Freiheit.

Galison für Schreibwaren, Designers Guild für Textilien und Tapeten, Vista Alegre für Porzellan, Roche Bobois für Möbel und Schmid für Küchen – worauf achten Sie, wenn Sie die Zusammenarbeit mit einer neuen Marke beginnen?
Da setzt der Instinkt ein, genau wie bei der Entscheidung zu einer romantischen Partnerschaft! Ich habe jede Menge Kriterien, die festlegen, ob ich mir eine neue Geschäftsbeziehung vorstellen kann. Eines der wichtigsten ist natürlich der spürbare, beidseitige Wunsch, etwas Neues, noch nie Dagewesenes zu erschaffen.

Sie arbeiten mit einem breiten Spektrum von Gegenständen – von Smartphone-Accessoires über Badezimmereinrichtung hin zu Tapeten, um nur einige zu nennen. Könnten Sie uns mehr über den kreativen Prozess erzählen, und darüber, wie Sie es schaffen, den Geist von Christian Lacroix in verschiedene Designs zu übertragen?
Ich habe das Glück, für eine Marke zu arbeiten, bei der Fantasie, Leichtigkeit und Kühnheit an erster Stelle stehen und bei einem breiten Publikum Anklang finden. Wir bekommen eine ganze Reihe von Angeboten aller Art und prüfen jedes davon sorgfältig. Wenn dann ein Produkt, auch ein unerwartetes, unsere Aufmerksamkeit erregt, überlegen wir gemeinsam, wie es in unsere Kollektionen aufgenommen werden kann. Unser einzigartiger Facettenreichtum ist der Hauptgrund, warum wir mit so vielen verschiedenen Partnern zusammenarbeiten können. Das ist auch der Grund, warum wir so bekannt und über die Generationen hinweg beliebt sind.

Was ist ihr Herzenswunsch für die Zukunft der Lifestylekollektionen von Lacroix?
Christian Lacroix Maison gibt es jetzt seit 13 Jahren. Und das verdanken wir allein unserer Vergangenheit. Wir haben, wenn auch auf ganz andere Weise, an eine Erfolgsgeschichte angeknüpft, die vor mehr als 35 Jahren begann. Ich hoffe, dass es diese Marke noch für lange Zeit geben wird. Was die Zukunft der Christian-Lacroix-Lifestylekollektionen angeht, so lasse ich mich am liebsten von einem unerwarteten Vorschlag überraschen, wie bei jenem Innenarchitekturprojekt für ein Luxusgebäude in Guatemala, an dem wir gerade gearbeitet haben. Das Leben ist voller Überraschungen – man muss nur darauf vertrauen.

Atelier Oï x Louis Vuitton

You have designed many objects for the Objets Nomades collection by Louis Vuitton. How did this fruitful collaboration start?

We started the collaboration a long time ago with the first object designed in 2011. We had a great chance, as this was the very beginning of the project Objets Nomades and Louis Vuitton was considering new products for their first collection, developing new markets, and doing research about different designers around the world. Now, the department responsible for this branch is quite important and successful but when we were invited to the project, it was not even called Objets Nomades; the designers only had the task of developing beautiful objects to travel with. Before designing our first contribution, we were invited to go to Asnières, near Paris, where Louis Vuitton had his private home and where he also started his company with a small atelier. The house is still there, full of objects that belonged to him and family memories. At that time a family member was still living there; now it is more a kind of museum, but with an active workshop. We visited this special place with a guide, who told us more about the Vuittons, and how they were collecting many beautiful objects. It was a real introduction to the history of the family and the essence of the company. We knew about Louis Vuitton before going there, but we knew it from the outside, as a great, impressive brand. Compared to our lifestyle, in a small village, we felt it would be a challenge to collaborate with such a major company but during the meeting at this house, something changed in our mind. We understood that it was a family business, that it had started small, and that the essence is still there – we can feel it. We had the chance to visit the first workshop, which is still there – the brand uses it for special orders,

and we were able to meet with all the craftspeople who still work there. This you cannot see in a shop: you would only see the products, but not necessarily the people behind them. To us it was quite important. As we experiment with materials, we are more "cooking" than designing, so it was good to see how they work with materials. We were impressed both by the family house and the way the craftspeople operated. To us it is important to touch, to feel, to see the craftspeople working and this is exactly what we discovered at the Asnières workshop. It was a completely big change in our mind.

As a collection of travel-inspired objects and furniture, Objets Nomades is quite special. What was most exciting for you in this concept?

It became emotional, and we wanted to develop projects, and leather objects to try to express the beauty of leather and the work of the craftsmen. These were our goals in this collaboration. At the beginning we did not have any precise brief, more a task to think about objects or pieces of furniture you can take with you on travel. It was true to the idea of Louis Vuitton collections that are marked by the idea of travelling. When we started to design, we thought of beautiful objects of the past century, which smart adventurers, mainly Englishmen, were travelling around the globe with. Beautiful objects, made of leather and other noble materials, and we were thinking of a similar collection for new, contemporary explorers. We began with a question of what would be the two objects we need to have for travel – we thought a place to sleep and a place to sit. So we came up with the idea of a folding chair or stool, and soon afterwards a hammock. We wanted them, particularly in the case of the folding chair, to look like a piece of luggage, an object that you can carry, handle. This was the first step of the development, and of course every object, for us, is the exploration of a material but also the story behind it. The first launch was in Miami in 2011 at the Art Basel Miami fair. Our hammock and the folding stool were presented with designs by the Campana brothers.

Were these first two designs for the Objets Nomades the most challenging ones?
For the folding stool we wanted it to be light – we were thinking of origami, the Japanese art of folding paper – and to create from a two-dimensional material a three-dimensional structure that would be static.
At the same time we were working on an exhibition and installations at the Mouvements Modernes gallery in Paris. The whole Louis Vuitton team visited the exhibition, and they were looking at the objects, saying, let's think about the hammock. To use leather and find a way to create a hammock – it seems to be an easy piece, but it was actually quite challenging. The folding stool was the first object, so it was challenging because it was at the beginning of the collaboration, but I think the hammock was even more challenging. When we started working with the material we thought it would be easy to use leather ribbons to create a hammock, but soon we understood that it was too hard, and thus not so comfortable. Generally, the question was not how to use leather in the structure, but how to create a structure with the leather. We were trying with several mock-ups, and once our design partner Armand came after lunch and he said he had cooked farfalle – the butterfly-like pasta. Its structure is just like a ribbon squeezed in the middle. As I said before, we like to see ourselves as cooks. We realised that cooked farfalle is smooth enough, so we tried to create farfalle with ribbons and we showed Louis Vuitton our prototype. This is an important part of our work, particularly in our collaboration with Louis Vuitton, that we experiment and create prototypes, we bring them to Paris and discuss them with the brand, and they try to make some changes if necessary. Now, after many, many years it is a close connection with their teams, who contribute to the creation.

How do you find working with leather?
It is almost the same in all the projects, the idea to twist the leather. We always try to create three-dimensional objects through tensions of the materials, not by putting forms inside the leather, but by twisting it. It is about pushing the limits of the material, just like when we were discussing how to fix and squeeze the leather for the hammock. That was at a time when Marc Jacobs was leading the fashion department and we met with some people from his team who told us about the fasteners on jeans – the rivets. We looked into the possibility of using them for the hammock and it helped us finalise the concept. It was challenging to develop an object that seems to be easy but requires a lot of attention to provide maximum comfort, and to use the leather in three dimensions. Using leather has been part of the brief, but we also have a fascination with the material.

Some designers use other materials, so the team at Louis Vuitton were not necessarily pushing for the leather.

How do you test your solutions and ideas?
We have equipped our studio for this purpose. This is why we never moved – we have kept this space, in the village, in the middle of nowhere. From the beginning we were always dealing with materials, with machines, as we are a workshop. We are inspired a lot by nature, and usually we find a structure by using the material. We like to keep all our tests, all our prototypes, as an archive of our experimental work. It is just like a cook trying a new recipe: he does not know what the result will be, but he wants to try the ingredients. It is also due to the fact that we are a collective studio, not a one-man show, so we like to think together. This is why the objects we create are not necessarily identifiable as one studio's works – because many designers work on them and bring their individuality to each project. The aesthetic expression is informed by the materials and by the structure.

What is the starting point of each design – are you given a theme, a kind of course to follow, or rather carte blanche?
It is a mutual inspiration. Sometimes when we had discovered a way to use the leather, we came up with new objects that we submitted to the team at Louis Vuitton, and sometimes they were inspired by our work. Once the architecture department saw our projects and they decided to use our approach for shop windows. So, we get inspired by them, and they by us. It can just happen that while playing with a material we start thinking about a possible use for a specific object, but typically with the lamps, it is a brief from the brand, because they are technically complex. If you want to sell worldwide, you have to be aware of all electric regulations – it requires know-how and a multidisciplinary team. And of course, the brief is about how to create a consistent universe for the client, so design has gradually become quite important. Briefs help us to understand what the clients expect and we also present the objects to their clients to learn more about their needs.

You work with various brands. How have you dealt with differences between design brands and couture houses in terms of thinking about objects for everyday use?
We see each collection as a universe of objects, from Atelier Oï and other designers. What is special in this collection is the fact that it is strongly related to the craftsmanship. We, the designers, have different backgrounds: the Campanas and Tokujin Yoshioka, we are all very different in our visions, but there is also a family of objects. Even if the aesthetic of the concept or the philosophy of each designer is different, it is quite interesting and special to see how you can mix the objects to organise the space and create an atmosphere. The objects are quintessentially Louis Vuitton, and you feel a common thread between them.

Sie haben viele Objekte für die Objets-Nomades-Kollektion von Louis Vuitton entworfen. Wie hat diese fruchtbare Zusammenarbeit begonnen?
Die Zusammenarbeit begann vor langer Zeit, das erste Objekt wurde schon 2011 entworfen. Wir hatten eine großartige Chance, da dies der Beginn von Objets Nomades war und Louis Vuitton über neue Produkte für die erste Kollektion nachdachte, neue Märkte erschließen wollte und sich über verschiedene Designerinnen und Designer aus der ganzen Welt informierte. Mittlerweile ist die Abteilung, die für den Ableger verantwortlich ist, ziemlich wichtig und erfolgreich, doch als wir zu dem Projekt eingeladen wurden, hieß es noch nicht einmal Objets Nomades; die Designer hatten lediglich die Aufgabe, schöne Objekte zum Reisen zu kreieren. Bevor wir unseren ersten Beitrag entwarfen, wurden wir nach Asnières in der Nähe von Paris eingeladen, in die private Residenz von Louis Vuitton, wo er in einem kleinen Atelier seine Firma gegründet hat. Das Haus ist immer noch da, voller persönlicher Gegenstände und Familienerinnerungen. Damals wohnte dort noch ein Familienmitglied; jetzt ist es eher eine Art Museum, aber mit einer aktiven Werkstatt. Wir besuchten diesen besonderen Ort mit einem Guide, der uns mehr über die Vuittons und ihre große Sammlung schöner Gegenstände erzählte. Es war ein toller Einblick in die Familiengeschichte und das Herzstück des Unternehmens. Wir kannten Louis Vuitton schon vorher, aber nur von außen, als diese großartige, beeindruckende Marke. Verglichen mit unserem Lebensstil in einem kleinen Dorf hatten wir das Gefühl, dass es eine Herausforderung wäre,

mit einem so großen Unternehmen zusammen-
zuarbeiten, aber während des Treffens in diesem
Haus änderte sich etwas an unserer Einstellung.
Wir verstanden, dass es ein Familienunternehmen war,
das klein angefangen hatte, und dass diese Essenz
immer noch vorhanden ist – das kann man spüren.
Es gibt die allererste Werkstatt noch, und wir hatten
die Gelegenheit, sie zu besuchen – die Firma nutzt
sie für Sonderanfertigungen, und wir konnten all die
Menschen treffen, die immer noch dort arbeiten. Das
können Sie in einem Geschäft nicht sehen: Sie sehen
nur die Produkte, aber nicht unbedingt die Menschen
dahinter. Für uns war das sehr wichtig. Während wir
mit Materialien experimentieren, „kochen" wir eher
als dass wir entwerfen, daher war es gut zu sehen,
wie sie mit den Materialien umgingen. Wir waren
sowohl vom Familienanwesen als auch der Arbeitsweise
der Designer sehr angetan. Für uns ist es wichtig
Dinge zu berühren, sie zu ertasten, den Künstlerinnen
und Künstlern bei der Arbeit zuzusehen, und genau
das war in der Werkstatt von Asnières möglich.
Es hat unser Denken vollkommen verändert.

    Thematisch sind die Objekte und Möbel der
    Kollektion von Objets Nomades vom Reisen
    inspiriert und ziemlich außergewöhnlich. Was
    hat Sie am meisten an dem Konzept fasziniert?
Es wurde zu einer Herzensangelegenheit, und wir
wollten Projekte aus Leder verwirklichen, die
die Schönheit des Materials und die handwerkliche
Arbeit hervorheben. Das waren unsere Ziele
bei dieser Kollaboration. Am Anfang gab es keine
genauen Vorgaben. Die Aufgabe lag eher darin, über
Ausrüstungsgegenstände nachzudenken,

die man mit auf Reisen nimmt. Das war ganz im Sinne
der Kollektionen von Louis Vuitton, die von der Idee
des Reisens geprägt sind. Als wir mit dem Entwerfen
anfingen, dachten wir an schöne Gegenstände des
vergangenen Jahrhunderts, mit denen gut ausgerüstete
Abenteurer, vor allem die Engländer, um den Globus
reisten. Wunderschöne Objekte, gefertigt aus Leder
und anderen edlen Materialien, und wir dachten
an eine vergleichbare Kollektion für neue, moderne
Entdeckerinnen und Entdecker. Wir begannen mit der
Suche nach den beiden Dingen, die man unbedingt
zum Reisen benötigt – und kamen zu dem Schluss,
dass dies ein Schlaf- und ein Sitzplatz wären. So kamen
wir auf die Idee eines Klappstuhls oder Hockers,
und bald darauf einer Hängematte. Sie sollten wie
ein Gepäckstück aussehen, vor allem der Klappstuhl;
wie ein Gegenstand, den man mit sich tragen kann.
Dies war der erste Schritt, und für uns geht es natürlich
bei jedem Objekt um das Spiel mit dem Material,
aber auch um die Geschichte dahinter. Unsere erste
Präsentation war 2011 in Miami, beim Art Basel Miami
Fair. Die Hängematte und der Klappstuhl wurden
mit Designs der Brüder Campana ausgestellt.

    Waren diese ersten beiden Entwürfe für die Objets
    Nomades am herausfordernsten?
Der Klappstuhl sollte leicht sein – wir dachten an
Origami, die japanische Papierfaltkunst – und wir
wollten aus einem zweidimensionalen Material eine
dreidimensionale Struktur schaffen, die tragfähig ist.
Gleichzeitig arbeiteten wir an einer Ausstellung und
Installationen in der Mouvements Modernes Gallery in
Paris. Das ganze Team von Louis Vuitton besuchte die
Ausstellung. Sie sahen die Gegenstände und meinten,

nun sei die Hängematte an der Reihe. Eine Hängematte aus Leder herzustellen scheint auf den ersten Blick leicht, aber tatsächlich war es ziemlich schwierig. Der Klapphocker war anspruchsvoll, weil er das erste Objekt war und die Zusammenarbeit begründete, aber ich denke, die Hängematte war die größere Herausforderung. Als wir mit der Arbeit anfingen, dachten wir, wir könnten einfach eine Hängematte aus Lederstreifen machen, doch bald erkannten wir, dass das Material zu hart und damit zu unbequem war. Im Endeffekt war die Frage nicht, wie man Leder in das Werk einfügt, sondern wie man mit dem Leder ein Werk erschafft. Wir haben verschiedene Modelle ausprobiert, und eines Tages kam unser Designpartner Armand nach dem Mittagessen zurück und erzählte, dass er Farfalle gekocht hatte – diese Pasta in Schmetterlingsform. Sie sieht aus wie ein Band, das in der Mitte zusammengedrückt wird. Wie ich schon sagte, wir betrachten uns gerne als Köche. Wir realisierten, dass gekochte Farfalle glatt genug sind, also kreierten wir Farfalle aus Lederbändern und zeigten Louis Vuitton den Prototyp. Dies ist ein wichtiger Teil unserer Arbeit, insbesondere in der Zusammenarbeit mit Louis Vuitton, dass wir experimentieren und Prototypen erstellen, sie nach Paris bringen, dem Unternehmen vorstellen und gegebenenfalls einige Änderungen vornehmen. Jetzt, nach diesen vielen Jahren, besteht eine enge Verbindung zu den Teams der Marke, und sie sind Teil des kreativen Prozesses.

Wie gefällt Ihnen die Arbeit mit Leder?
Die Idee, das Leder zu verdrehen, ist bei allen Projekten ähnlich. Unser Ziel ist immer, durch Spannungen im Material dreidimensionale Objekte zu schaffen, nicht indem wir Formen in das Leder einarbeiten, sondern indem wir es drehen und zwirbeln. Es geht darum, die Grenzen des Materials auszuloten, genau wie damals bei der Hängematte, als wir nach einigem Ausprobieren zu der Lösung mit dem Zusammendrücken kamen. Zu der Zeit leitete Marc Jacobs die Modeabteilung, und wir trafen uns mit einigen Leuten aus seinem Team, die uns von der Verstärkung der Jeansnähte durch Nieten erzählten. Wir überlegten, wie wir das für die Hängematte nutzbar machen konnten, und es half uns dabei, zu einer finalen Lösung zu kommen. Es war eine Herausforderung und viel Arbeit, ein scheinbar so einfaches Objekt zu entwickeln, das aus dreidimensionalem Leder gefertigt ist und maximalen Komfort bietet. Die Verwendung von Leder war Teil des Auftrags, aber wir sind von dem Material auch fasziniert. Einige Designer verwenden andere Materialien, daher drängte das Team von Louis Vuitton nicht unbedingt auf das Leder.

Wie testen Sie Ihre Ideen?
Im Studio, genau dafür ist es ausgestattet. Deshalb sind wir nie umgezogen – wir haben diesen Raum behalten, im Dorf, mitten im Nirgendwo. Von Anfang an haben wir uns immer mit den Materialien, mit den Maschinen beschäftigt, da wir eine Werkstatt sind. Wir lassen uns gerne von der Natur inspirieren, und indem wir das Material verwenden, finden wir

normalerweise die Form. Die Ergebnisse unserer Tests, die ganzen Prototypen, bewahren wir als ein Archiv unserer experimentellen Arbeit auf. Es ist wie bei einem Koch, der ein neues Rezept ausprobiert: Er weiß nicht, was das Ergebnis sein wird, aber er möchte die Zutaten probieren. Das liegt auch daran, dass wir ein Studiokollektiv sind, keine Ein-Mann-Show, wir denken also gerne gemeinsam nach. Deshalb sind die von uns geschaffenen Objekte nicht unbedingt als Werke eines einzigen Studios identifizierbar – weil viele Designer daran arbeiten und ihre Individualität in jedes Projekt einbringen. Der ästhetische Ausdruck wird durch die Materialien und die Struktur bestimmt.

Was ist der Ausgangspunkt jedes Designs – gibt man Ihnen ein Thema, einen Kurs vor, dem Sie folgen, oder haben Sie vollkommen freie Hand?
Es ist eine gegenseitige Inspiration. Manchmal fanden wir einen neuen Weg, das Leder zu verarbeiten, und entwarfen neue Objekte, die wir dem Team von Louis Vuitton vorstellten, und manchmal wurden sie von unserer Arbeit inspiriert. Einmal sah die Architekturabteilung unsere Projekte und entschied sich, diesen Ansatz bei den Schaufenstern zu verwenden. Also, wir werden von ihnen inspiriert, und sie von uns. Es kann einfach passieren, dass uns beim Spielen mit einem Material eine mögliche Verwendung für ein bestimmtes Objekt einfällt. Nur bei den Lampen, die technisch komplex sind, gibt es im Regelfall Vorgaben von der Firma. Wenn Sie weltweit verkaufen wollen, müssen Sie die elektrischen Vorschriften aller Länder kennen – das erfordert Know-how und ein multidisziplinäres Team. Und natürlich geht es darum, einen Wiedererkennungswert für die Kundschaft zu schaffen, daher ist das Design im Laufe der Zeit sehr wichtig geworden. Vorgaben können uns helfen zu verstehen, was die Kundinnen und Kunden erwarten, und wir präsentieren ihnen die Gegenstände auch, um mehr über ihre Wünsche zu erfahren.

Sie arbeiten mit verschiedenen Marken zusammen. Wie gehen Sie mit Unterschieden zwischen Designern und Modehäusern um, wenn es um das Nachdenken über Alltagsgegenstände geht?
Wir betrachten jede Kollektion als ein Universum von Objekten, von Atelier Oï und anderen Designern. Das Besondere an dieser Kollektion ist die Tatsache, dass sie eng mit dem Handwerk verknüpft ist. Wir, die Designer, haben ganz verschiedene Hintergründe: die Campanas und Tokujin Yoshioka haben unterschiedliche Visionen, doch es gibt auch Gegenstände, die miteinander in Beziehung treten. Auch wenn die Ästhetik oder die Philosophie der Designer unterschiedlich ist, kann es sehr interessant und besonders sein, die Objekte zu mischen, um den Raum zu strukturieren und eine gewisse Atmosphäre zu schaffen. Alle Objekte sind typisch Louis Vuitton, und man spürt die Verbindung zwischen ihnen.

LEISURE
FREIZEIT

CHRISTIAN LACROIX FOR GALISON, PLAYING CARDS BY PHILIPPE GARCIA
CHRISTIAN LACROIX FÜR GALISON, SPIELKARTEN VON PHILIPPE GARCIA

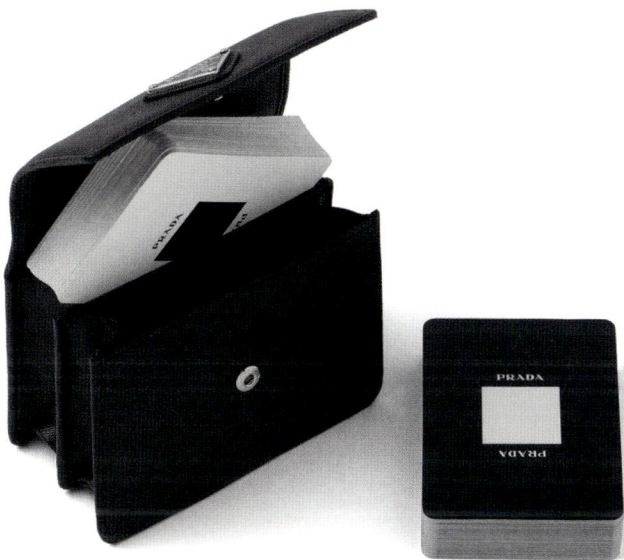

DIOR, PLAYING CARDS CASE
DIOR, BOX MIT SPIELKARTEN

PRADA, SAFFIANO LEATHER
CASE WITH PLAYING CARDS
PRADA, ETUI AUS SAFFIANO-LEDER
MIT SPIELKARTEN

Game club
Game club

Whether lavishly packed or decorated with
a dose of eccentricity, these sets take playing
cards to a new level. Elegant simplicity
or original fantasy infuse traditional games
with playfulness as well as style.

Ob aufwendig verpackt oder exzentrisch
verziert: diese Sets heben Spielkarten
auf ein neues Level. Schlichte Eleganz
oder originelle Fantasiewelten bringen
Leichtigkeit und Stil in altbekannte Spiele.

PRADA, SAFFIANO
LEATHER POKER SET
PRADA, POKER-SET AUS
SAFFIANO-LEDER

BACCARAT, POKER CARDS
BACCARAT, POKER KARTENSPIEL

DIOR, POKER SET
DIOR, POKER-SET

>
SUPREME, GOLD FOIL
PLAYING CARDS
SUPREME, SPIELKARTEN
MIT GOLDBESCHICHTUNG

James Bond's favourite game is gaining
popularity among professional players and
cards aficionados. High bids, exciting risks,
and a lot of suspense require an elegant
setting. Why not raise the stakes with
a gilded set?

Ob aufwendig verpackt oder exzentrisch
verziert: diese Sets heben Spielkarten
auf ein neues Level. Schlichte Eleganz
oder originelle Fantasiewelten bringen
Leichtigkeit und Stil in altbekannte Spiele.

Games for two players – from the red-and-black checkers from Prada, with their striking minimalism, to the lesser known Chinese Mahjong game based on tile-like elements, and Go, a board game requiring a strategist's brain that is said to be more difficult than chess.

Spiele für zwei Personen – vom auffallend minimalistischen, rot-schwarzen Damespiel von Prada über das weniger bekannte chinesische Mahjong-Spiel, das mit sogenannten Ziegeln gespielt wird, bis hin zu Go, einem Brettspiel für echte Strategen, das schwieriger sein soll als Schach.

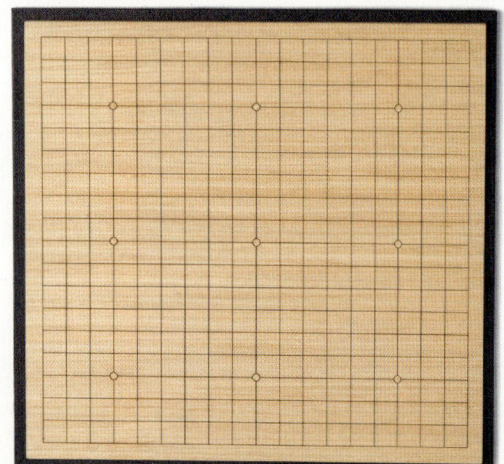

PRADA, SAFFIANO LEATHER CHECKERS SET
PRADA, DAME–SET AUS SAFFIANO-LEDER

PRADA, SAFFIANO LEATHER MAHJONG GAME
PRADA, MAHJONG-SPIEL AUS SAFFIANO-LEDER

> PRADA, SAFFIANO LEATHER GO SET
PRADA, GO–SET AUS SAFFIANO-LEDER

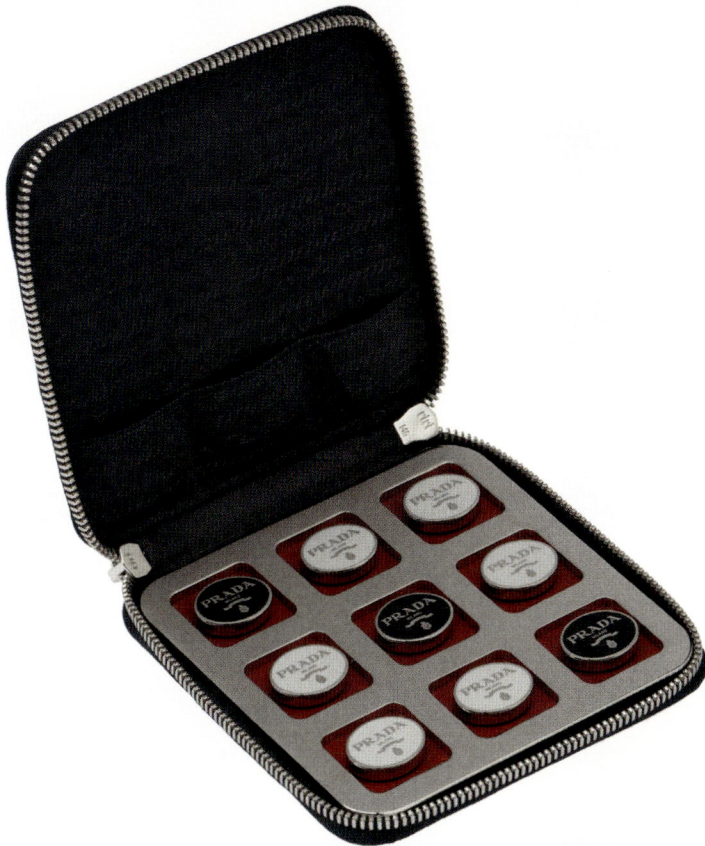

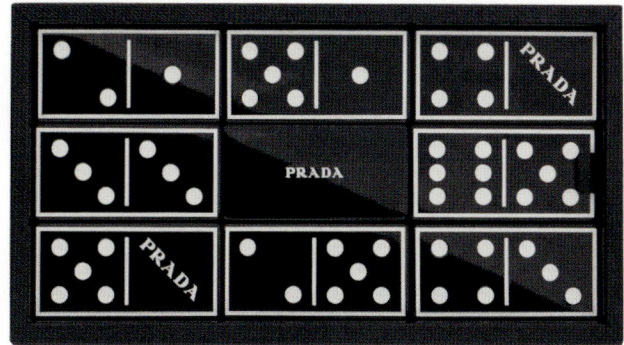

Anyone who thought of these two traditional games as boring will change their mind after playing with these sets. Dominoes – in classic black-and-white or made of oak wood – will awaken many memories, while the Tic-Tac-Toe from Prada in an elegant leather case with a zipper can be easily taken along on the go.

Jeder, der diese beiden traditionellen Spiele für langweilig hielt, wird seine Meinung ändern, nachdem er mit diesen Sets gespielt hat. Das Dominospiel – in klassischem Schwarz-Weiß oder aus Eichenholz – wird viele Erinnerungen wecken, während das Tic-Tac-Toe-Spiel von Prada im eleganten Lederetui mit Reißverschluss bequem unterwegs mitgenommen werden kann.

PRADA, SAFFIANO LEATHER
TIC-TAC-TOE
PRADA, TIC-TAC-TOE-SET
AUS SAFFIANO-LEDER

PRADA, SAFFIANO LEATHER
DOMINOES SET
PRADA, DOMINO-SET
AUS SAFFIANO-LEDER

<
DIOR MAISON X PIERRE
YOVANOVITCH, DOMINOES
DIOR MAISON X PIERRE
YOVANOVITCH, DOMINOSTEINE

VERSACE, MEDUSA
TIC-TAC-TOE SET
VERSACE, MEDUSA
TIC-TAC-TOE-SET

VERSACE, BAROCCO
DOMINO SET
VERSACE, BAROCCO
DOMINO-SET

Versace realises these traditional games
in an XL format, which transforms them
into accessories that, in addition
to entertainment, are also elements
of decoration. Embellished with the brand's
iconic Medusa symbol, they come in
a distinctive colour palette.

Von Versace stammen diese traditionellen
Spiele im XL-Format, die damit zu
Accessoires werden und neben der
Unterhaltung auch zur Dekoration dienen.
Sie sind mit der ikonischen Medusa der
Marke verziert und in charakteristischen
Farbkombinationen erhältlich.

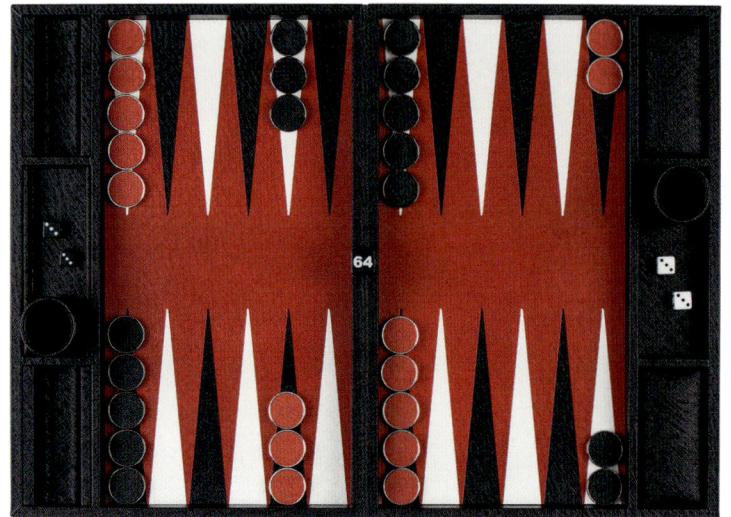

PRADA, SAFFIANO LEATHER
BACKGAMMON SET
PRADA, BACKGAMMON-SET
AUS SAFFIANO-LEDER

DIOR, LARGE EMBROIDERED
BACKGAMMON
DIOR, GROSSES BESTICKTES
BACKGAMMON

CHOPARD, BACKGAMMON
CLASSIC RACING
CHOPARD, CLASSIC RACING
BACKGAMMON-SET

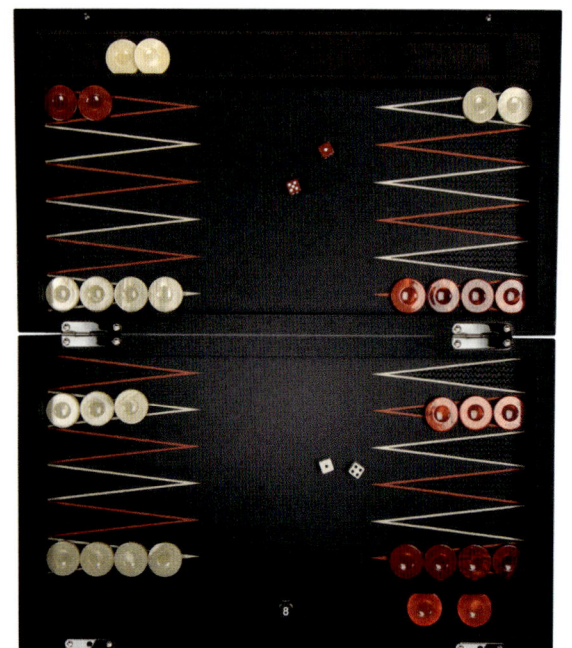

CHRISTIAN LACROIX FOR GALISON,
BACKGAMMON BY PHILIPPE GARCIA.
CHRISTIAN LACROIX FÜR GALISON,
BACKGAMMON-SET VON PHILIPPE GARCIA.

Two pairs of dice, a doubling cube, two
dice cups for shaking, and the characteristic
board – in short Backgammon, a game with
centuries-old traditions. These masterly
crafted Backgammon sets with brands'
signature motifs and noble materials,
like wood, leather, and embroidery, are like
pieces of art and true objects of desire.

Zwei Würfelpaare, ein Dopplerwürfel,
zwei Würfelbecher und das charakteristische
Brett – kurz: Backgammon, ein Spiel
mit jahrhundertealter Tradition. Diese
meisterhaft gefertigten Backgammonsets
mit markentypischen Motiven und aus
edlen Materialien wie Holz, Leder
und Stickereien sind echte Kunstwerke
und wahre Objekte der Begierde.

BACCARAT, CHESS GAME
BACCARAT, SCHACHSPIEL

ZAHA HADID DESIGN, FIELD OF TOWERS CHESS SET
ZAHA HADID DESIGN, FIELD OF TOWERS SCHACH-SET

Shared moments are even more
sophisticated over a game of chess.
Although it is timeless, its traditions
can be revisited in some of the most
original ways. Baccarat delights with refined
forms and the pure beauty of clear and
Midnight crystal, which play with the light
with striking visual effects (all pieces are cut
by hand). Zaha Hadid Design introduces
a lacquered and polished chess board with
a silk-screen printed grid and polished resin
sculptural pieces that are informed by
the architect's signature dynamic twists.
The elaborately painted porcelain figures
from Nymphenburg are safely enveloped
in an classic case. For fans of modernity,
Prada's quietly luxurious version is another
great choice.

Gemeinsame Augenblicke werden noch
bedeutsamer bei einer Partie Schach.
Obwohl das Spiel zeitlos ist, kann es
auf bemerkenswert originelle Arten neu
interpretiert werden. Baccarat begeistert mit
raffinierten Formen und der reinen Schönheit
von klarem und mitternachtsblauem Kristall,
in dem sich effektvoll das Licht bricht (alle
Stücke werden von Hand geschliffen). Von
Zaha Hadid Design stammt das lackierte und
polierte Schachbrett mit Siebdruckmuster
und skulpturalen Figuren aus poliertem
Kunstharz, die die charakteristisch
geschwungenen Linien der Architektin
aufgreifen. Die aufwendig glasierten
Porzellanfiguren von Nymphenburg werden
sicher in einem klassischen Etui aufbewahrt.
Für Fans von modernem Design ist die
unaufgeregt luxuriöse Variante von Prada
ebenfalls eine gute Wahl.

PORZELLAN MANUFAKTUR
NYMPHENBURG, CHESS
BOARD WITH FIGURINES
PORZELLAN MANUFAKTUR
NYMPHENBURG,
SCHACHSPIEL INKLUSIVE
FIGUREN

PRADA, SAFFIANO
LEATHER CHESS SET
PRADA, SCHACH-SET AUS
SAFFIANO-LEDER

Tables to play
Spieltische

The perforated monogram leather net
and ten balls with the Louis Vuitton logo
embraced by a leather strap give this
numbered edition table an iconic touch.
Equipped with two drawers for the four
rackets, it has beechwood legs with
adjustable feet. The table is available
in two sizes – domestic as well as professional.

Das perforierte Netz aus Leder mit
Monogramm-Motiv und die zehn Bälle
mit dem Louis-Vuitton-Logo, die von
einem Lederriemen gehalten werden,
machen diesen Tisch in limitierter Auflage
zum Kultobjekt. Er ist ausgestattet mit
zwei Schubladen für vier Schläger, sowie
höhenverstellbaren Beinen aus Buchenholz.
Der Tisch ist in zwei Größen erhältlich –
sowohl für den häuslichen als auch
für den professionellen Gebrauch.

LOUIS VUITTON, PING-PONG TABLE CANVAS
LOUIS VUITTON, TISCHTENNISTISCH MIT CANVAS

The vintage style VVT Foosball Table is wrapped in the signature pattern made of the Monogram Flower and a Louis Vuitton engraving. The craftsmanship expressed in the hand-painted players and leather-coated handles make it a powerful piece that will add a touch of class, and fun, to any interior.

Der Tischkicker im Vintage-Stil ist mit einem Muster aus der charakteristischen Monogrammblume bezogen und hat die Louis-Vuitton-Signatur eingraviert. Die Handwerkskunst, die in den hand-bemalten Spielern und lederbezogenen Griffen zum Ausdruck kommt, macht den Tisch zu einem kraftvollen Statement, das jedem Innenraum einen Hauch von Klasse und Verspieltheit verleiht.

LOUIS VUITTON, VVT FOOSBALL TABLE
LOUIS VUITTON, BABYFOOT CANVAS

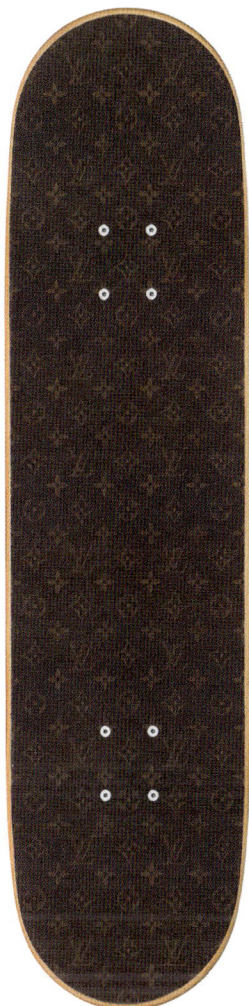

Skatepark adventure
Abenteuer Skatepark

From a sports activity for youngsters to a strong component of street art culture, skateboarding has become popular among many. Traversing pavement or performing tricks in a skatepark can be quite impressive, especially when using the perfect skateboard. Luxury brands have made a special nod to the enthusiasts of outdoor sports and have turned the skateboard into a collector's item.

Sei es als sportliche Aktivität für Jugendliche oder als bedeutender Bestandteil der Streetart-Kultur; Skateboarding ist bei vielen beliebt. Durch die Straßen zu fahren oder Tricks in einem Skatepark vorzuführen sorgt schnell für bewundernde Blicke, erst recht mit dem perfekten Skateboard unter den Füßen. Luxusmarken haben ein besonderes Augenmerk auf die Liebhaber von Outdoor-Sportarten gelegt und das Skateboard zu einem Sammlerstück gemacht.

VERSACE, BAROCCO SKATEBOARD
VERSACE, BAROCCO SKATEBOARD

LOUIS VUITTON, MONOGRAM SKATEBOARD
LOUIS VUITTON, MONOGRAMM-SKATEBOARD

GUCCI, GUCCI LOGO SKATEBOARD IN BLACK WOOD
GUCCI, SKATEBOARD MIT GUCCI-LOGO AUS SCHWARZEM HOLZ

Beach time
Strandzeit

One cannot imagine better leisure time than a day spent on the beach. Luxury brands have made sure to provide all possible accessories to make these moments a great pleasure. Sporting activities bring many opportunities for playful designs, like a racket to play padel, a sport that combines aspects of tennis, squash, and badminton. Versace lovers can go to the beach fully equipped with uniform style accessories including this extraordinary inflatable swimming ring.

Man kann sich keine bessere Freizeitbeschäftigung vorstellen als einen Tag am Strand. Luxusmarken stellen alle denkbaren Accessoires bereit, um diese Zeit zum größten Vergnügen zu machen. Verschiedene Sportarten bieten viele Möglichkeiten für verspielte Designs, wie zum Beispiel einen Schläger für Padel, einer Sportart, die Elemente aus Tennis, Squash und Badminton miteinander verbindet. Versace-Liebhaber können sich voll ausgestattet mit Accessoires im einheitlichen Stil, einschließlich dieses außergewöhnlichen aufblasbaren Schwimmrings, am Strand blicken lassen.

VERSACE: CRETE DE FLEUR INFLATABLE FLOAT, CRETE DE FLEUR BEACH TOWEL, CRETE DE FLEUR BEACH RACKET SET,
VERSACE: CRETE DE FLEUR AUFBLASBARER SCHWIMMRING CRETE DE FLEUR STRANDTUCH, CRETE DE FLEUR STRANDSCHLÄGER–SET

>
PRADA, PADEL RACKET
PRADA, PADELSCHLÄGER

At the pool
Am Pool

Exteta, the Italian brand designing and producing luxury and high-performing furniture, has teamed up with French fashion designer Simon Porte Jacquemus to create a special re-edition of Gae Aulenti's renowned Locus Solus collection.
"The series hails from Gae Aulenti's 1960s pop production and combines strong lines with vintage charm, enhancing harmony and versatility in space," explains the manufacturer. The pieces from the collection, including a sun lounger and armchair, are available in an off-white structure with a yellow-striped textile finish.

Exteta, die italienische Marke, die hochwertige Luxusmöbel entwirft und herstellt, hat sich mit dem französischen Modedesigner Simon Porte Jacquemus zusammengetan, um eine einzigartige Neuauflage der berühmten Locus Solus Kollektion von Gae Aulenti zu entwerfen. „Die Serie stammt aus Gae Aulentis Pop-Phase in den 1960er Jahren und kombiniert starke Linien mit Vintage-Charme, was die Harmonie und Wandelbarkeit des gestalteten Raumes hervorhebt", erklärt das Unternehmen. Die Stücke aus der Kollektion, darunter eine Sonnenliege und ein Stuhl, sind in einer beigefarbenen Struktur mit gelb gestreiftem Textilfinish erhältlich.

JACQUEMUS + EXTETA, LOCUS SOLUS COLLECTION
JACQUEMUS + EXTETA, LOCUS SOLUS KOLLEKTION

Following the continuous trend of enjoying
the pleasures of outdoor living, numerous
luxury brands have launched objects
as well as pieces of furniture for everyday
use that demonstrate unique craftsmanship
and the signature features of each house.
FENDI Casa offers a sun lounger with
contemporary lines, while Gubi combines
durable Iroko wood with high-performance
polyester rope. The lightweight Palaver chair
has been envisioned by Patricia Urquiola
for the Objets Nomades collection. Made
of 150 strips of cowhide leather woven
onto the solid oak frame, it is foldable.
The meticulous structure of the leatherwork
is enhanced by its vivid blue hue.

Dem anhaltenden Trend folgend, die
Freuden des Lebens im Freien zu genießen,
haben zahlreiche Luxusmarken Gegenstände
und Möbelstücke für den alltäglichen
Gebrauch auf den Markt gebracht, die das
einzigartige handwerkliche Können und die
charakteristischen Merkmale jedes Hauses
zum Ausdruck bringen. FENDI Casa bietet
eine Sonnenliege mit zeitgemäßen Linien,
Gubi hingegen kombiniert strapazierfähiges
Iroko-Holz mit hochwertigen Polyesterseilen.
Der leichte Palaver Chair wurde von Patricia
Urquiola für die Objets Nomades Kollektion
entworfen. Er ist zusammenklappbar und
besteht aus 150 Streifen Rindsleder, die auf
den massiven Eichenrahmen gewebt sind.
Die filigrane Lederarbeit wird durch den
intensiven blauen Farbton noch verstärkt.

FENDI CASA, KATHY SUNBED
BY PALOMBA SERAFINI
FENDI CASA, KATHY SONNENLIEGE
VON PALOMBA SERAFINI

LOUIS VUITTON, PALAVER CHAIR
BY PATRICIA URQUIOLA
LOUIS VUITTON, PALAVER CHAIR
VON PATRICIA URQUIOLA

<
GUBI, MR01 OUTDOOR LOUNGE CHAIR
BY MATHIAS RASMUSSEN
GUBI, MR01 OUTDOOR-LOUNGESESSEL
VON MATHIAS RASMUSSEN

Accessories for outdoor living are usually defined by a vibrant palette of hues and dynamic patterns, like in the Missoni Home series of outdoor seats, poufs, and cushions in Nastri Jacquard fabric, available in various shapes and sizes, or in the bathrobe featuring the brand's iconic zigzag motif. In the collection by Raf Simons for Kvadrat, including beach towels and bathrobes, the colours are enhanced by the textured Jacquard pattern.

Outdoor-Accessoires stechen häufig durch eine lebendige Farbauswahl und dynamische Muster hervor, so auch bei den Outdoor-Stühlen, Polsterhockern und Nastri-Kissen aus Jacquard-Stoff von Missoni Home, die in verschiedenen Formen und Größen erhältlich sind, oder beim Bademantel mit dem ikonischen Zickzackmuster der Marke. In der Kollektion von Raf Simons für Kvadrat, die Strandtücher und Bademäntel enthält, werden die Farben durch das strukturierte Jacquardmuster hervorgehoben.

KVADRAT/RAF SIMONS,
SHAKER SYSTEM
KVADRAT/RAF SIMONS,
SHAKER SYSTEM

MISSONI HOME, CECIL
HOODED BATHROBE
MISSONI HOME, CECIL
BADEMANTEL MIT KAPUZE

<
MISSONI HOME COLLECTION 2023
MISSONI HOME COLLECTION 2023

Eating al fresco
Essen al fresco

Italian *al fresco* translates to 'in the fresh air', emblematic of nice weather and a vacation-like atmosphere. To celebrate special moments of enjoying a meal outdoors, these two wicker baskets can help create a romantic and stylish picnic for up to four. Marcel Wanders employs an original shape which allows the limited size. Miss Dior's basket includes dinner and dessert plates, coffee ware, crystal glasses, and olive-wood silverware, as well as napkins, a jacquard tablecloth, and a wool and cashmere blanket. For less bucolic solo meals, Prada offers a luxurious yet very practical picnic bag equipped with everything necessary.

Italienisch *al fresco* bedeutet übersetzt , „an der frischen Luft", und steht sinnbildlich für schönes Wetter und Urlaubsstimmung. Für besondere Mahlzeiten im Freien gelingt mit diesen beiden Weidenkörben ein romantisches und stilvolles Picknick für bis zu vier Personen. Marcel Wanders verwendet eine originelle Form, die die platzsparende Größe ermöglicht. Der Korb von Miss Dior umfasst Ess- und Dessertteller, Kaffeegeschirr, Kristallgläser und Besteck aus Olivenholz sowie Servietten, eine Jacquard-Tischdecke und eine Decke aus Wolle und Kaschmir. Für weniger pastorale, einfache Mahlzeiten bietet Prada eine luxuriöse und dennoch sehr praktische Picknicktasche, die mit allem Notwendigen ausgestattet ist.

ALESSI, 'DRESSED EN PLEIN AIR' PICNIC BASKET BY MARCEL WANDERS
ALESSI, PICKNICKKORB ‚DRESSED EN PLEIN AIR' VON MARCEL WANDERS

>

DIOR, MISS DIOR PICNIC BASKET
DIOR, MISS DIOR PICKNICKKORB

PRADA, PICNIC BAG
PRADA, PICKNICKTASCHE

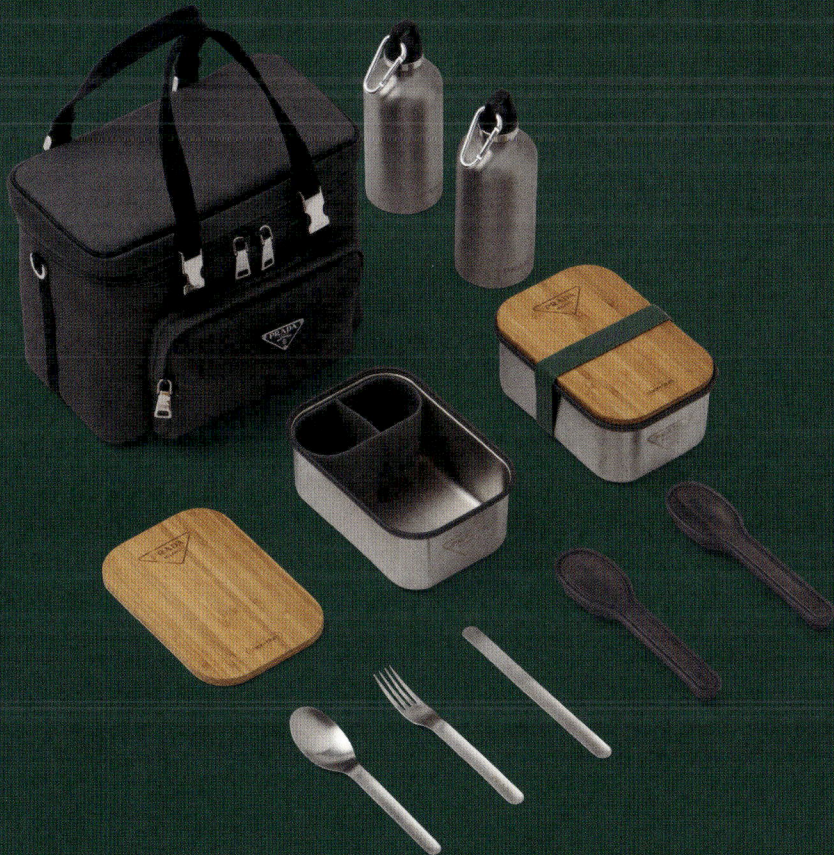

SPORTS
SPORT

Let's go to the gym!
Ab ins Fitnessstudio!

The dream of having a private gym
at home is closer than one may think with
this elegant set from Ethimo, the universal
design of which can complement all kinds
of architecture. Envisioned by Studio Adolini
for a perfect workout outdoors, it also
connects with the landscape and nature.
Enjoy an open-air spot for exercising
the body and relaxing the mind!

Der Traum von einem privaten Fitnessstudio
zu Hause rückt mit diesem eleganten Set von
Ethimo, dessen universelles Design zu allen
erdenklichen Arten von Architektur passt,
näher, als man denkt. Konzipiert von
Studio Adolini für ein perfektes Workout
im Freien, schafft es auch eine Verbindung
zur Landschaft und zur Natur. Erfreuen
Sie sich an einem Platz unter freiem
Himmel, zum körperlichen Training
und zur geistigen Entspannung!

OUT-FIT, ETHIMO AND STUDIO ADOLINI
OUT-FIT, ETHIMO UND STUDIO ADOLINI

DIOR, FITNESS SET
DIOR, FITNESS-SET

LOUIS VUITTON,
DUMBBELLS 2 KG
LOUIS VUITTON, 2 KG
SCHWERE HANTELN

>
PRADA, JUMP ROPE
PRADA, SPRINGSEIL

PRADA, RE-NYLON
AND SAFFIANO LEATHER
HAND WEIGHTS
PRADA, HANDGEWICHTE
AUS RE-NYLON UND
SAFFIANO-LEDER

For indoor fitness, luxury brands offer a wide range of chic exercise equipment. Thanks to their sophisticated forms and noble materials, these items also make a physical workout into an aesthetic experience. Stretching, toning muscles, exercising with dumbbells, or jumping with these exquisite instruments all improve the well-being of the body in grand style.

Für Indoor-Fitness bieten Luxusmarken eine große Auswahl an schicken Trainingsutensilien an. Durch die raffinierten Formen und edlen Materialien machen diese Artikel auch ein körperliches Training zum ästhetischen Erlebnis. Ob Stretching, Muskelaufbau, Hanteltraining oder Springen, diese exquisiten Geräte verbessern das körperliche Wohlbefinden im großen Stil.

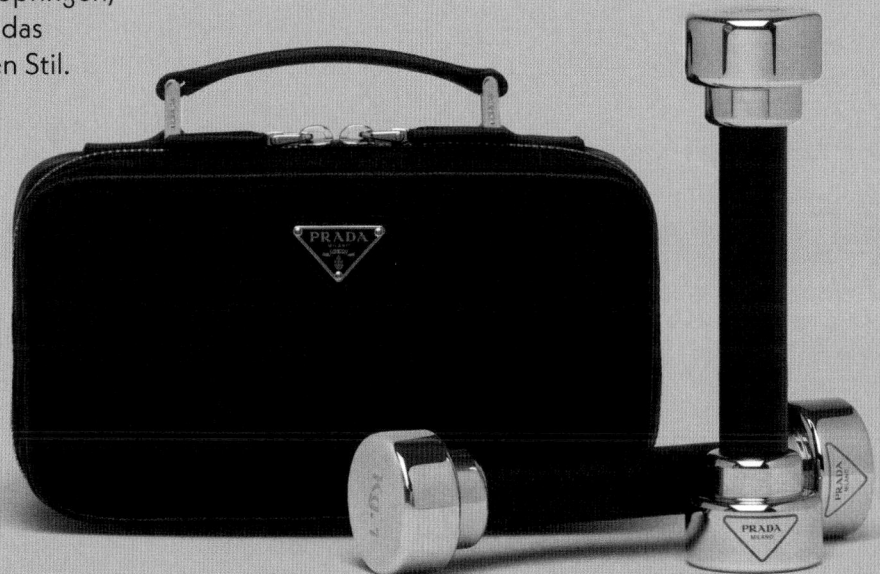

The pleasure of sliding
Die Freude am Gleiten

Eco-sustainable materials, high-level performance, and cutting-edge design that makes manoeuvres easy and fun, not to mention eye-catching style – this is officially the ultimate paradise for skiers and snowboarders. Accented with brands' emblematic patterns, the luxurious equipment perfectly matches the techwear collection.

Ökologisch nachhaltige Materialien, hohe Leistungsfähigkeit und innovatives Design machen jedes Fahrmanöver zum reinsten Vergnügen; dazu ein Style, der die Aufmerksamkeit aller auf sich lenkt – das beschreibt wohl den ultimativen Traum aller Ski- und Snowboardfahrenden. Akzentuiert durch die wiedererkennbaren Muster der unterschiedlichen Marken, passt das luxuriöse Equipment perfekt zur Techwear-Kollektion.

DIOR, SNOWBOARD
DIOR, SNOWBOARD

PRADA, LINEA ROSSA
SNOWBOARD AND SKIS>
PRADA, LINEA ROSSA
SNOWBOARD UND SKIER>

>
LOUIS VUITTON,
MONOGRAM STRIPE SKIS
LOUIS VUITTON, SKIER MIT
MONOGRAMM UND STREIFEN

This versatile kit for skiing and snowboarding from Dior arrives in a vivid blue that beautifully echoes the clear winter sky and will certainly draw attention on the slopes! Enhanced by the latest safety innovations, the accessories have been envisioned for the highest-quality comfort. The signature CD diamond is a discreet final touch.

Dieses vielseitige Kit zum Skifahren und Snowboarden von Dior spiegelt das leuchtende Blau des klaren Winterhimmels auf unvergleichliche Weise wider und wird auf den Pisten mit Sicherheit Aufmerksamkeit erregen! Das Zubehör ist auf dem neuesten Stand der Sicherheitstechnik und wurde für höchsten Komfort konzipiert. Der unverkennbare CD-Diamant gibt dem Ganzen einen diskreten letzten Schliff.

DIOR AND POC, GOOGLES, GLOVES AND HELMET
DIOR UND POC, BRILLE, HANDSCHUHE UND HELM

Dior teamed up with Rimowa to design a perfect carry-on suitcase for frequent travelers. Made of ultra-light aluminium, the shell is extremely hard-wearing. With four wheels for smooth movements, it also has handles on the top and side for vertical and horizontal carrying. The Dior Oblique pattern is like the cherry on the cake.

Dior hat sich mit Rimowa zusammengetan und einen perfekten Handgepäckkoffer für Vielreisende entworfen. Die Schale aus ultraleichtem Aluminium ist extrem strapazierfähig. Der Koffer hat vier Rollen für bessere Beweglichkeit und Griffe sowohl oben als auch an der Seite, um ihn quer und hochkant tragen zu können. Für das gewisse Etwas sorgt schließlich das Dior-Oblique-Motiv.

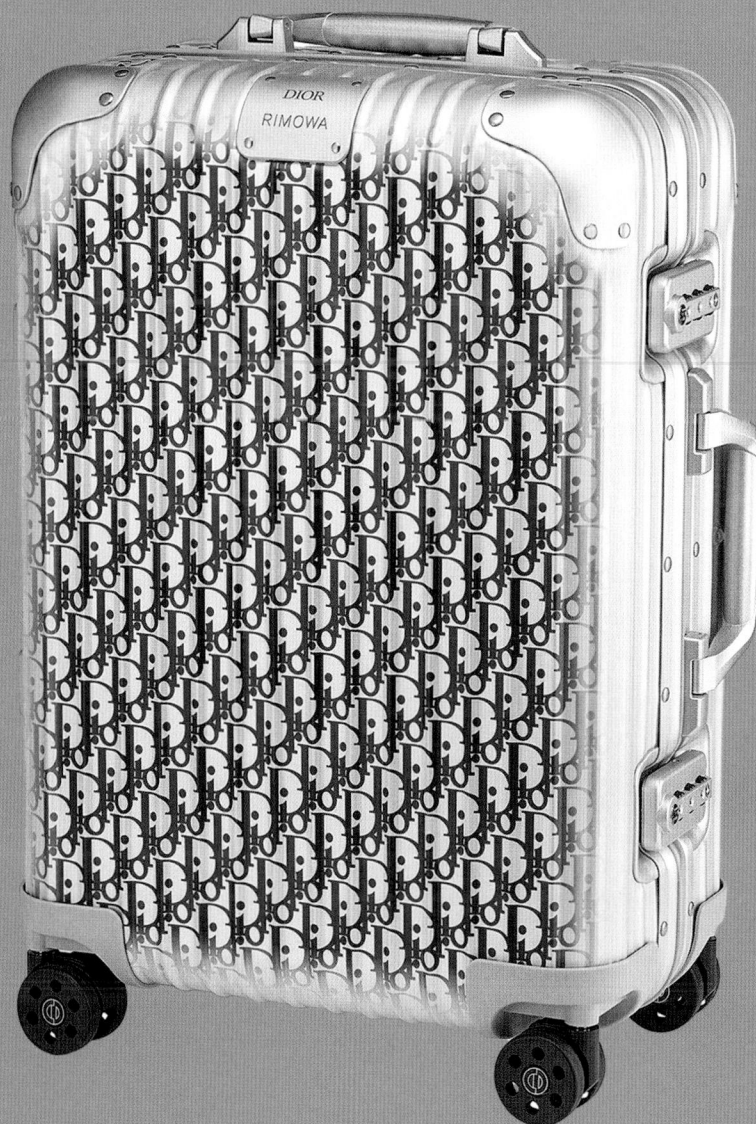

DIOR AND RIMOWA, CABIN SUITCASE
DIOR UND RIMOWA, KABINENKOFFER

Supreme has collaborated with top brands to create some of the most extraordinary luggage pieces. The large rectangular bag with a shoulder strap and vivid red leather handles, a team-up with Louis Vuitton, and their playful aluminium suitcases released together with Rimowa cannot go unnoticed. These make the perfect companions for travel and luxury aficionados!

Supreme hat mit Top-Marken zusammengearbeitet, um einige der außergewöhnlichsten Gepäckstücke zu kreieren. Die große rechteckige Tasche mit Schulterriemen und leuchtend roten Ledergriffen, eine Kollaboration mit Louis Vuitton, und die verspielten Aluminiumkoffer, die zusammen mit Rimowa herausgebracht wurden, stechen sofort ins Auge. Es sind die perfekten Begleiter für Reise- und Luxusliebhaber!

RIMOWA X SUPREME, SUITCASES
RIMOWA X SUPREME, KOFFER

<
SUPREME X LOUIS VUITTON, HOLDALL
SUPREME X LOUIS VUITTON, REISETASCHE

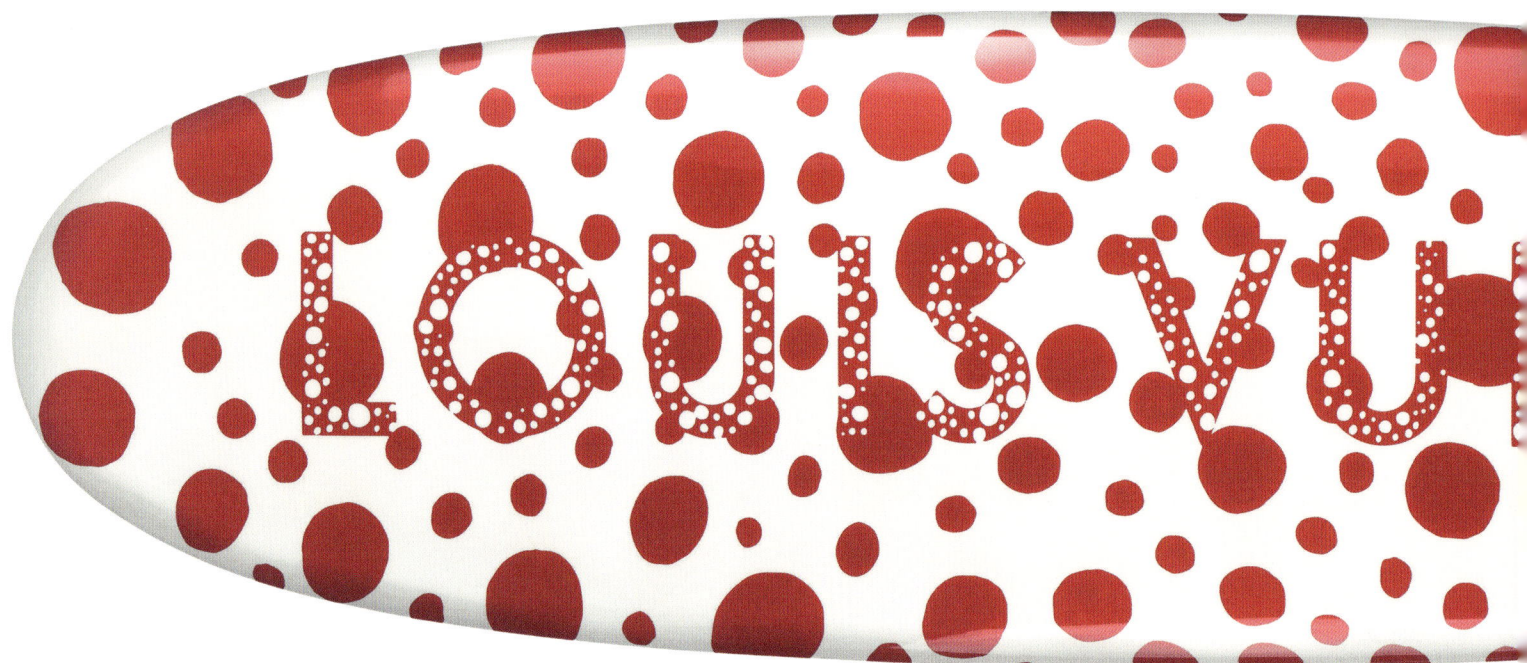

Going with the waves
Auf den Wellen reiten

Designed as a tribute to Yayoi Kusama's Yellow Pumpkin and as part of the famous collaboration between Louis Vuitton and the Japanese artist, these surfboards are a special limited edition. The high-end, artisanal surfboard is made of fibreglass, resin, and basswood and is available in two sizes – a regular one and a sporty shortboard size.

Diese Surfbretter sind eine limitierte Sonderedition, entworfen als Hommage an Yayoi Kusamas gelben Kürbis und Teil der fruchtbaren Zusammenarbeit zwischen Louis Vuitton und der japanischen Künstlerin. Das hochwertige, handgefertigte Surfbrett besteht aus Glasfaser, Harz und Lindenholz und ist in zwei Größen erhältlich – als universelles Brett und als sportives Shortboard.

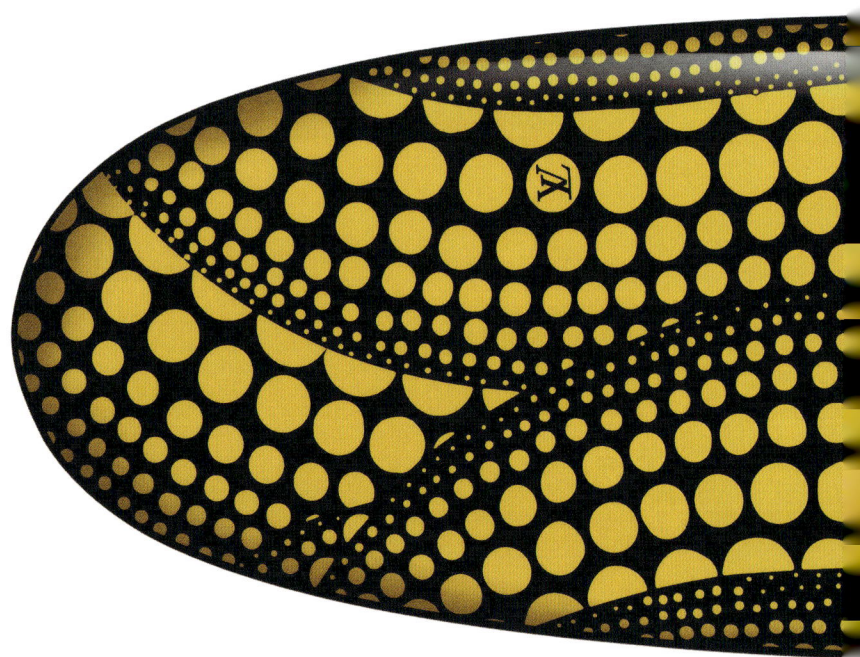

LOUIS VUITTON, LV X YK SURF
LOUIS VUITTON, LV X YK SURFBRETT

Featuring brands' iconic patterns and colours (which are often combined with matching sportswear) and made of high-quality materials, these mats will certainly please yoga enthusiasts. Ideal for training at home or at the gym, for stretching or meditation, they are equipped with comfortable carrying straps.

An diesen Matten, mit den ikonischen Mustern und Farben der Marken und aus hochwertigen Materialien gefertigt (oft kombinierbar mit passender Sportbekleidung), finden Yoga-Enthusiastinnen und -Enthusiasten sicherlich Gefallen. Sie eignen sich ideal für das Training zu Hause oder im Studio, zum Dehnen oder Meditieren, und sind mit bequemen Tragegurten ausgestattet.

BOSS, YOGA MAT WITH SIGNATURE-STRIPE STRAP
BOSS, YOGAMATTE MIT CHARAKTERISTISCH GESTREIFTEM TRAGEGURT

VERSACE, YOGA MAT CRETE DE FLEUR
VERSACE, YOGAMATTE CRETE DE FLEUR

PRADA, YOGA MAT
PRADA, YOGAMATTE

Roll the ball
Der Ball rollt

Versace knows how to take basketball and football to a new level. The Barocco pattern covering the entire surface of the balls turns them into surprising, beautiful objects – that at the first glance do not look like typical balls at all – and puts them in the middle of the game.

Versace versteht es, Basketball und Fußball auf ein neues Level zu heben. Das Barocco-Muster, das die gesamte Oberfläche der Bälle bedeckt, verwandelt diese in wunderschöne Objekte – die auf den ersten Blick überhaupt nicht wie typische Bälle aussehen – und macht sie zum Mittelpunkt des Spiels.

VERSACE, BAROCCO
BASKETBALL AND
FOOTBALL
VERSACE, BASKETBALL
UND FUSSBALL BAROCCO

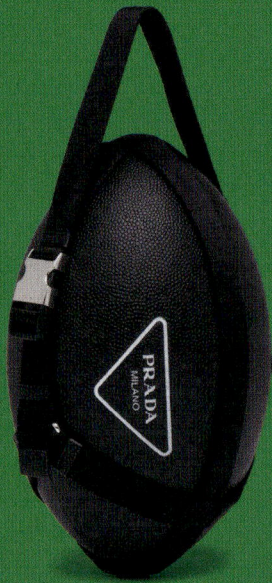

For fans of sports and outdoor activities,
Prada offers a whole collection of balls
for different disciplines as collectors' items.
The comfortable nylon band harness with
a side-release buckle makes carrying them
to the pitch very easy. Whether in classic
black and red colours or in a colourful palette
recalling a summer atmosphere, their only
decorative element is the brand's logo.
Last but not least, Prada offers a stylish set
for the famous French outdoor game Boules.
The balls, made of resin, are enveloped with
a sophisticated carrying case of luxurious
Saffiano leather.

Für Sport- und Outdoor-Fans bietet
Prada eine ganze Kollektion von Bällen für
verschiedene Disziplinen als Sammlerstücke
an. Mit dem komfortablen Nylongurt mit
seitlicher Schnalle kann man sie bequem
zum Spielfeld tragen. Das einzige dekorative
Element ist das Markenlogo, das sowohl
auf den Bällen in klassischem Schwarz oder
Rot als auch auf der farbenfrohen Variante
prangt, die sogleich Sommergefühle weckt.
Zu guter Letzt bietet Prada ein stilvolles
Set für das berühmte französische Outdoor-
Spiel Boule. Die Kugeln aus Kunstharz
werden in einer edlen Tragevorrichtung
aus luxuriösem Saffiano-Leder transportiert.

PRADA, RESIN BOCCE SET
PRADA, BOCCIA-SET AUS HARZ

<

PRADA, FROM THE LEFT: RUGBY,
SAFFIANO LEATHER SOCCER BALL,
BASKETBALL, VOLLEYBALL
PRADA, VON LINKS: RUGBYBALL,
FUSSBALL AUS SAFFIANO-LEDER,
BASKETBALL, VOLLEYBALL

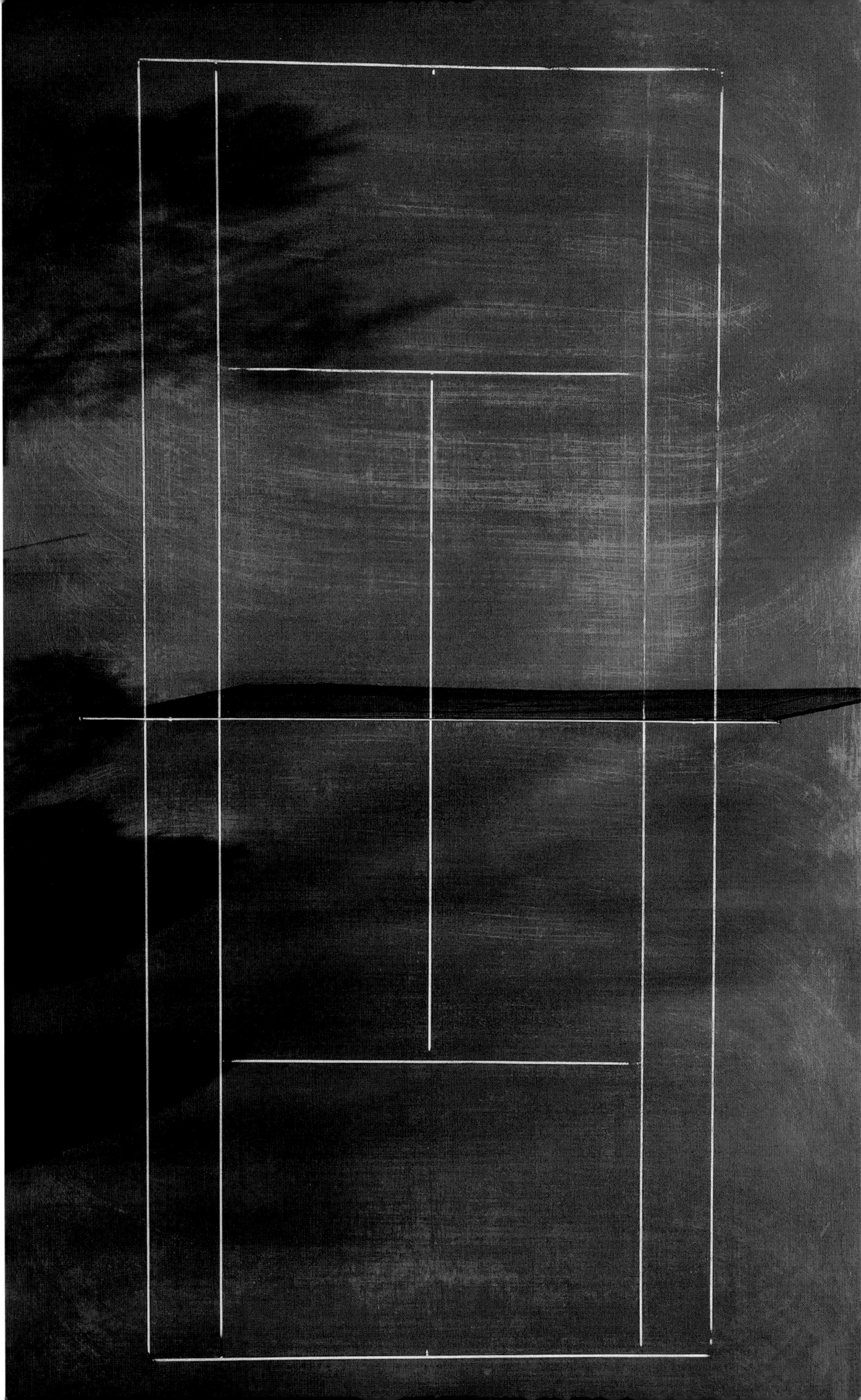

Game, set, match
Spiel, Satz, Sieg

PRADA, TENNIS RACKET
AND TENNIS BALL CASE
PRADA, TENNISSCHLÄGER
UND TENNISBALL-HÜLLE

Envisioned in line with the sleek aesthetics
of Prada, this black tennis racket is classic and
elegant. Stored in a Re-Nylon case made
of recycled plastic, as is the set of branded
tennis balls, it is a stylish reason for another
tennis match.

Dieser schwarze Tennisschläger wurde im
Einklang mit der schlanken Ästhetik von
Prada im klassischen, eleganten Design
entworfen. Aufbewahrt wird er, ebenso
wie das Set von Tennisbällen mit
Markenlogo, in einer Hülle aus Re-Nylon
(recycelter Kunststoff) und ist ein stilvoller
Grund für ein weiteres Tennismatch.

limonium

OBJECTS
OBJEKTE

A drink to go
Getränke to go

Louis Vuitton presents an iconic cup in an eco-friendly and reusable version – a combination of porcelain and a natural cowhide Monogram Canvas sleeve for easy carrying and comfortable use. Equally stylish is the Flask Holder, equipped with a carrying strap and inspired by the nomadic spirit of the brand. The chic, steel engraved bottle keeps drinks warm or cool. The Dior Aqua Bottle also has a removable and adjustable shoulder strap. Designed in stainless steel, it features isothermal technology to keep drinks hot for 12 hours and cool for 24, as the brand specifies. The aluminium Travel Mug from Versace with a reusable straw is suitable for cold drinks and shines with its meticulous crystal embellishments.

DIOR, AQUA BOTTLE WITH SHOULDER STRAP
DIOR, TRINKFLASCHE MIT SCHULTERRIEMEN

VERSACE, CRYSTAL MEDUSA TRAVEL CUP
VERSACE, REISEBECHER CRYSTAL MEDUSA

Louis Vuitton präsentiert einen ikonischen Becher in einer umweltfreundlichen und wiederverwendbaren Version – eine Kombination aus Porzellan und einem Monogramm-Canvas-Sleeve aus naturbelassenem Rindsleder für einfaches Tragen und bequemen Gebrauch. Ebenso stilvoll ist der Flaschenhalter, der mit einem Tragegurt ausgestattet und vom nomadischen Geist der Marke inspiriert ist. Die schicke, mit Stahl gravierte Flasche hält Getränke warm oder kalt. Die Trinkflasche von Dior hat ebenfalls einen abnehmbaren und verstellbaren Schultergurt. Sie besteht aus Edelstahl und ermöglicht dank der isothermischen Technologie, Getränke 12 Stunden lang warm und 24 Stunden lang kalt zu halten, so die spezifischen Angaben des Unternehmens.
Der Aluminium-Reisebecher von Versace mit wiederverwendbarem Strohhalm eignet sich für kalte Getränke und besticht durch seine detailverliebten Kristallverzierungen.

CHOPARD, HAPPY BEAR
FORK AND SPOON BABY SET
CHOPARD, HAPPY BEAR
BABYSET MIT GABEL UND LÖFFEL

Children's universe
Kinderwelt

The golden teddy bear symbolic of Chopard adorns this silver cutlery set, with a nicely shaped spoon and fork, for baby's first meals, which comes in elegant case. The first dinner set from Dior includes a plate, a bowl, and a tumbler, all in extra fine Limoges porcelain, as well as four stainless steel utensils adapted for small hands. Stored in a colourful wooden valise, it can be a lovely gift for a first birthday. All elements are decorated with Dior's iconic Toile de Jouy motif, reimagined by Cordelia de Castellane. The motif also appears, engraved, on the silver-finish metal box for the precious baby tooth collection.

Dieses silberne Besteckset ziert der goldene Teddybär, ein bei Chopard gern verwendetes Symbol. Es wird im eleganten Etui geliefert und besteht aus einem schön geformten Löffel und einer Gabel für die ersten Mahlzeiten des Babys. Das erste Tafelservice von Dior umfasst einen Teller, eine Schale und einen Becher aus extra feinem Limoges-Porzellan sowie vier Edelstahl-Besteckteile für kleine Hände. Das Service, das in einem bunten Holzkoffer verstaut wird, ist eine schöne Geschenkidee für einen ersten Geburtstag. Alle Teile des Sets sind mit dem ikonischen Toile de Jouy-Motiv von Dior verziert, das von Cordelia de Castellane neu interpretiert wurde. Dasselbe Motiv findet sich auch als Gravur auf der Metaldose in Silber-Finish für die kostbare Milchzahnsammlung.

DIOR, MY FIRST DINNER SET
DIOR, MEIN ERSTES SERVICE

DIOR, BABY TOOTH BOX
DIOR, MILCHZAHNDOSE

A child's universe would not be complete without two characteristic objects – a piggy bank and a snow globe. In envisioning both, Versace employs the iconic Medusa head with a very stylish and decorative result, especially thanks to the gold coating (they are made of porcelain with a metallic finish).

Die Welt der Kinder wäre nicht komplett, wenn zwei typische Gegenstände fehlten – ein Sparschwein und eine Schneekugel. Für beides verwendet Versace den ikonischen Medusenkopf, was zu überaus stilvollen und dekorativen Ergebnissen führt, insbesondere dank der Goldbeschichtung (die Objekte bestehen aus Porzellan mit metallischem Finish).

VERSACE, GOLDEN MEDUSA SNOW GLOBE
VERSACE, SCHNEEKUGEL GOLDEN MEDUSA

VERSACE, BREAK THE BANK MONEY BOX
VERSACE, SPARBÜCHSE BREAK THE BANK

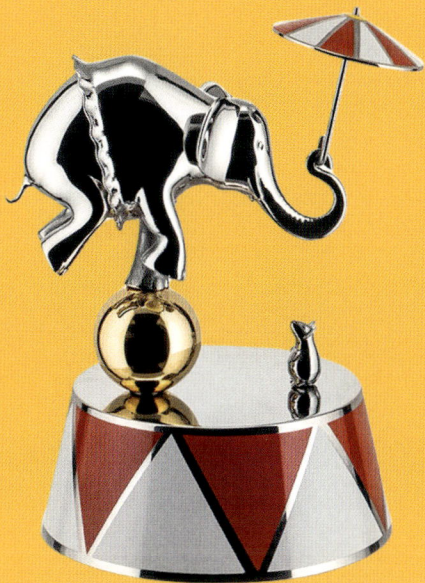

The Circus collection is a family of sculpture-
like collectors' objects, including a musical
box, a call bell, and a candy dispenser,
each limited to 999 copies and designed
with elements of fantasy. The playful forms
here meet the vivid colour decorations,
contrasting with the steel, often reflective,
surface to create striking visual effects.
Just like in a circus world!

Die Circus Collection besteht aus einer
Gruppe skulpturaler Sammlerobjekte,
darunter eine Spieldose, eine Tischschelle
und ein Bonbonspender, die jeweils auf 999
Exemplare limitiert und fantasievoll gestaltet
sind. Verspielte Formen treffen hier auf
lebhafte Farben, die mit den spiegelblanken
Stahloberflächen kontrastieren und auf diese
Weise auffällige visuelle Effekte erzielen.
Genau wie im Zirkus!

ALESSI, CIRCUS COLLECTION BY MARCEL WANDERS:
BALLERINA MUSICAL BOX, RINGLEADER CALL BELL,
AND CANDYMAN CANDY DISPENSER
ALESSI, CIRCUS COLLECTION VON MARCEL WANDERS,
HIER: SPIELDOSE BALLERINA, TISCHSCHELLE
RINGLEADER UND BONBONSPENDER CANDYMAN

Modes of Storage
Aufbewahrungsarten

These original containers in luxury versions
are elements that add chic as well as humour
to any interior. Jaime Hayon juxtaposes
exquisite crystal with a porcelain base
in a fanciful shape. Daniel Libeskind, true
to his domain, infuses an everyday object
with the power of architectonic structure
and selects an intriguing form, typical of
New York City's urbanscape.

Diese Luxusversionen origineller Behälter
verleihen jedem Innenraum mondänen
Charme und Humor. Jaime Hayon
stellt in fantasievoller Formvollendung
einen exquisiten Kristalldeckel einem
Porzellansockel gegenüber. Daniel
Libeskind, seiner Domäne treu, haucht
einem Alltagsgegenstand Leben ein,
indem er eine faszinierende architektonische
Form wählt, die sofort an die Stadtlandschaft
New York Citys denken lässt.

ALESSI, WATER TOWER
BY DANIEL LIBESKIND
ALESSI, WATER TOWER
VON DANIEL LIBESKIND
<
BACCARAT, ZOO COLLECTION
BY JAIME HAYON, FROG BOX
BACCARAT, ZOO COLLECTION
VON JAIME HAYON, FROSCHDOSE

This Change Tray and Oval Box feature
striking, curvaceous shapes inspired by the
jewellery collection designed by Delfina
Delettrez Fendi. The colour-block effect is
highlighted by the use of refined leather,
while the iconic FF metal embellishment is
another decorative element.

Das Tablett und die ovale Schachtel zeichnen
sich durch auffällige, geschwungene
Formen aus, die von Delfina Delettrez
Fendis Schmuckkollektion inspiriert sind.
Der Colour-Block-Effekt wird durch die
Verwendung von feinstem Leder noch
verstärkt, während die ikonische FF-
Metallverzierung ein weiteres
dekoratives Element darstellt.

FENDI CASA, O'LOCK
OVAL BOX
FENDI CASA, O'LOCK
OVALE SCHACHTEL

FENDI CASA, O'LOCK
CHANGE TRAY
FENDI CASA, O'LOCK
OVALES TABLETT

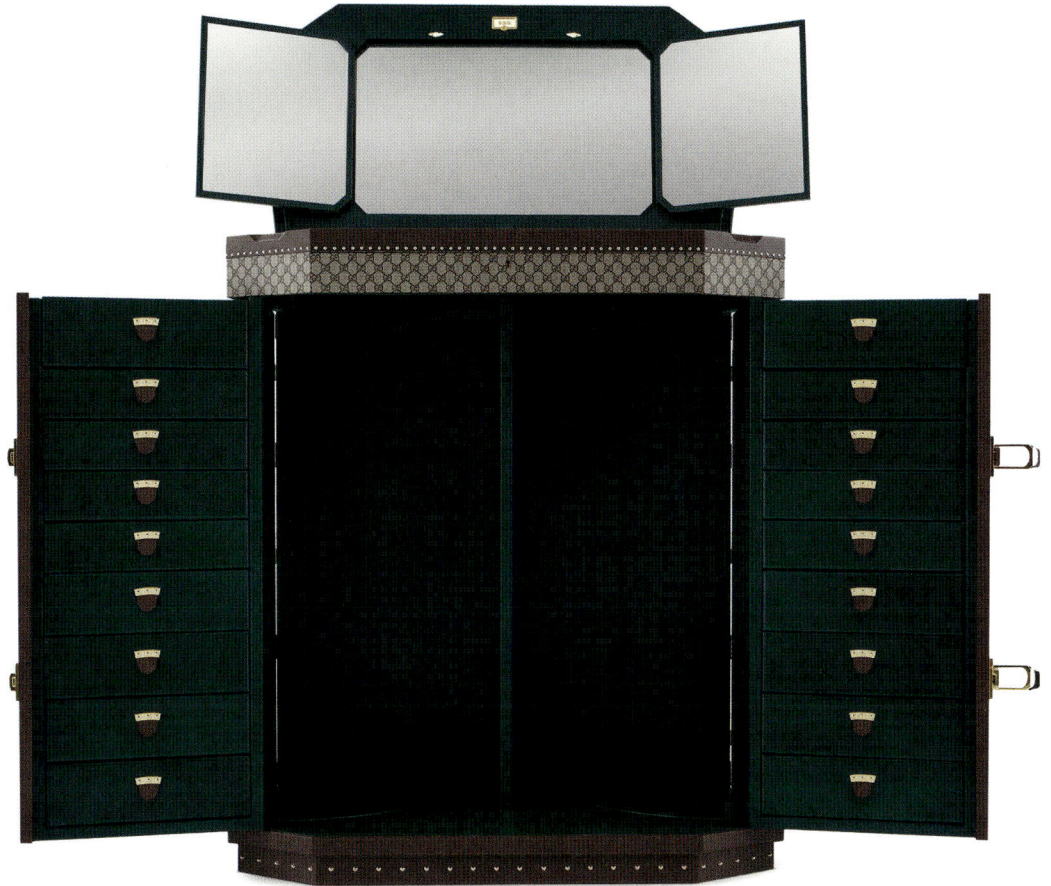

This impressive trunk is a homage to Guccio Gucci's beginnings as a porter at a London hotel. Its multiple drawers can be customised to contain jewels and watches, while a double lock with a key reveals a folding mirror at the top.

Dieser imposante Koffer ist eine Hommage an Guccio Guccis Anfänge als Portier in einem Londoner Hotel. Seine vielen Schubladen können individuell angepasst und zur Aufbewahrung von Schmuck und Uhren verwendet werden; im oberen Teil versteckt sich außerdem hinter einem Doppelschloss mit Schlüssel ein Klappspiegel.

GUCCI, GG SUPREME
JEWELLERY TRUNK
GUCCI, SCHRANKKOFFER
AUS GG SUPREME MIT
SCHMUCKSCHUBLADEN

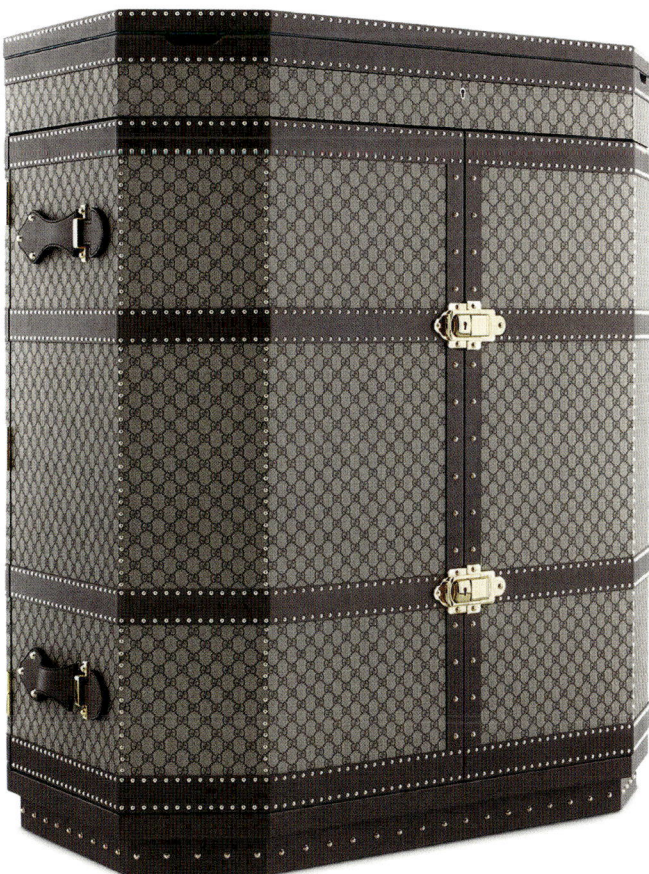

At the desk
Am Schreibtisch

The collaboration between Dior Maison and Pierre Yovanovitch resulted in a rich collection of objects, like a bookend, paperweight, and pencil holder, among others. In the spirit of minimal elegance, they are made of solid oak wood, highlighting their distinctive shapes.

Die Zusammenarbeit zwischen Dior Maison und Pierre Yovanovitch führte zu einer stattlichen Sammlung von Objekten, darunter eine Buchstütze, ein Briefbeschwerer und ein Stifthalter. Ganz im Geiste minimalistischer Eleganz sind sie aus massivem Eichenholz gefertigt, was die unverwechselbaren Formen besonders zur Geltung bringt.

DIOR MAISON X PIERRE YOVANOVITCH, PAPER-WEIGHT, BOOKEND, PENCIL HOLDER, TRINKET TRAY
DIOR MAISON X PIERRE YOVANOVITCH, BRIEFBESCHWERER, BUCHSTÜTZE, STIFTHALTER, SCHMUCKSCHALE

The dynamic play of black, red, and white triangles, so much part of Prada's identity, transforms flat catchall trays or simplistic boxes into vibrant objects and precious décor elements, which are also perfectly functional.

Das dynamische Zusammenspiel von schwarzen, roten und weißen Dreiecken, die so vollkommen zur Identität von Prada gehören, verwandelt flache Ablageschalen oder schlichte Schachteln in lebendige Objekte und kostbare Dekorelemente, die noch dazu funktional sind.

PRADA, RECTANGULAR PORCELAIN CATCHALL TRAYS
PRADA, RECHTECKIGE ABLAGESCHALEN AUS PORZELLAN

PRADA, WOOD AND SAFFIANO LEATHER BOX
PRADA, BOX AUS HOLZ UND SAFFIANO-LEDER

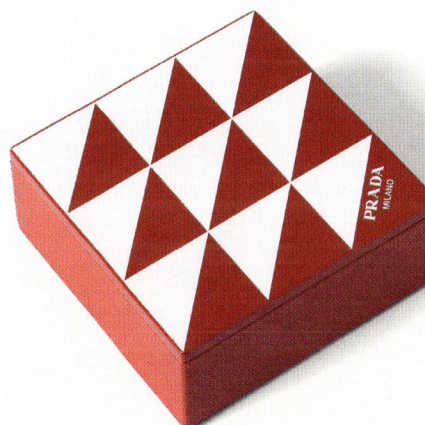

As part of Kvadrat's Shaker System collection, Raf Simons has designed a series of intriguing accessories that are reduced to their essence and executed in pure leather. The designer finds novel and striking solutions for ordinary objects, like the vertical magazine holder with two straps and five slides.

Als Teil der Shaker-System-Kollektion von Kvadrat hat Raf Simons eine Reihe faszinierender Accessoires entworfen, die aufs Wesentliche reduziert und ganz aus Leder hergestellt sind. Der Designer findet neuartige und erstaunliche Lösungen für gewöhnliche Objekte, wie den vertikalen Zeitschriftenhalter aus zwei Riemen und fünf verschiebbaren Trennelementen.

KVADRAT/RAF SIMONS, LEATHER MAGAZINE STRAP,
LEATHER MIRROR TRAY, LEATHER KEY CHAIN, VIDAR
KEY CHAIN
KVADRAT/RAF SIMONS, LEDERZEITSCHRIFTENHALTER,
LEDERSPIEGELTABLETT, LEDERSCHLÜSSELANHÄNGER,
VIDAR-SCHLÜSSELANHÄNGER

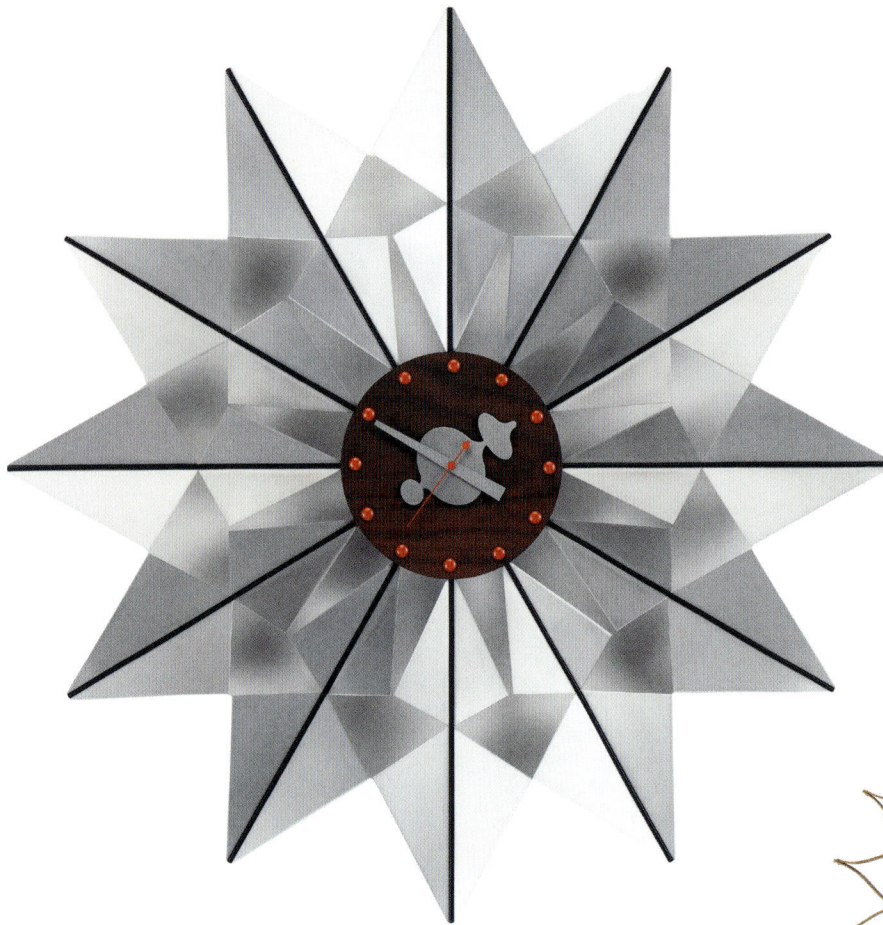

VITRA, WALL CLOCKS – FLOCK
OF BUTTERFLIES AND SUNFLOWER
CLOCK BY GEORGE NELSON
VITRA, WANDUHREN – FLOCK OF
BUTTERFLIES UND SUNFLOWER
CLOCK VON GEORGE NELSON

Tick Tock
Tick Tack

While watches naturally belong to the luxury department, clocks that indicate time in offices and homes around the globe are often unjustly overlooked. The one designed by Virgil Abloh was used as the invitation (in a limited edition of 1200 units) to his AW20 Louis Vuitton fashion show, while Vitra has re-issued some of the most precious wall clocks by the American designer George Nelson, which characteristically do not use numbers.

Armbanduhren zählen ohne Frage zu den Luxusobjekten, doch Wanduhren, die weltweit in Büros und Wohnungen die Zeit anzeigen, werden zu Unrecht häufig übersehen. Dieses von Virgil Abloh entworfene Exemplar diente als Einladung zu seiner HW20-Modenschau bei Louis Vuitton (in einer limitierten Auflage von 1200 Stück), während Vitra einige der wertvollsten Wanduhren des amerikanischen Designers George Nelson neu aufgelegt hat, die charakteristischerweise keine Zahlen verwenden.

LOUIS VUITTON, WALL CLOCK BY VIRGIL ABLOH
LOUIS VUITTON, WANDUHR VON VIRGIL ABLOH

Among many luxurious accessories in Chopard's palette, the clocks occupy a special place. Far from obvious, their watches magically change contexts and scales. A desk clock can be stylishly inspired by a dashboard counter or informed by the shape of an elegant wrist watch, only far larger.

Unter den vielen luxuriösen Accessoires von Chopard nehmen die Uhren einen besonderen Platz ein. Auf ganz erstaunliche, fast magische Weise verändern die Uhren des Unternehmens Kontexte und Maßstäbe. Eine Tischuhr kann stilvoll vom Zeitzähler am Armaturenbrett oder von der Form einer eleganten Armbanduhr inspiriert sein, nur weitaus größer.

CHOPARD, VINTAGE RACING TABLE CLOCK
CHOPARD, TISCHUHR VINTAGE RACING

CHOPARD, CLASSIC TABLE CLOCK
CHOPARD, CLASSIC TISCHUHR

<
CHRISTIAN LACROIX, IDYLLE EN VOL
A5 NOTEBOOK BY NEIL BICKNELL
CHRISTIAN LACROIX, A5 NOTIZ-
BUCH IDYLLE EN VOL VON NEIL
BICKNELL

CHRISTIAN LACROIX, ORCHID'S
MASCARADE CARDS BY NEIL
BICKNELL
CHRISTIAN LACROIX, KARTEN
ORCHID'S MASCARADE VON NEIL
BICKNELL

CHRISTIAN LACROIX, LES SAISONS
LACROIX BY PHILIPPE GARCIA
CHRISTIAN LACROIX, LES SAISONS
LACROIX VON PHILIPPE GARCIA

>
BOSS, CAMEL FAUX-LEATHER A5
NOTEBOOK WITH SIGNATURE
STRIPE STRAP
BOSS, KAMELFARBENES A5-
NOTIZBUCH AUS KUNSTLEDER MIT
CHARAKTERISTISCH GESTREIFTEM
BAND

Making a note
Notierenswert

Stationery is yet another realm where luxury
brands are brimming with ideas. Writing
greeting cards or filling notebooks has never
been so chic – from the rich patterns, joyful
colour palette, and original binding,
to the minimalist look, focusing on
the brands' emblems.

Schreibwaren sind ein weiterer Bereich,
in dem Luxusmarken voller Ideen
stecken. Grußkarten schreiben oder
Notizbücher füllen war noch nie so schick
– von überbordenden Mustern, fröhlichen
Farbpaletten und originellen Bindungen bis
hin zum minimalistischen Look, der sich auf
die Embleme der Marken konzentriert.

Collectibles for design aficionados
Sammlerstücke für Designliebhaber

For over two decades, the Vitra Design Museum has been producing miniature replicas of some of the most iconic pieces of their esteemed collection to illustrate milestones in furniture design. These precious pieces are quite striking thanks to the scale of the details – the grain in the wood, tiny screws, and textile textures are all meticulously reproduced.

Seit über zwei Jahrzehnten produziert das Vitra Design Museum Miniaturnachbildungen von einigen der ikonischsten Stücke seiner geschätzten Sammlung, um Meilensteine des Möbeldesigns zu würdigen. Diese kostbaren Stücke fallen dank ihrer detailgetreuen Nachbildung wirklich ins Auge – die Maserung im Holz, winzige Schrauben und die Texturen verschiedener Stoffe sind alle akribisch reproduziert.

VITRA, MINIATURES COLLECTION,
VITRA DESIGN MUSEUM, 1820–2011

VITRA, MINIATURES COLLECTION,
VITRA DESIGN MUSEUM, 1820–2011

PETS
HAUSTIERE

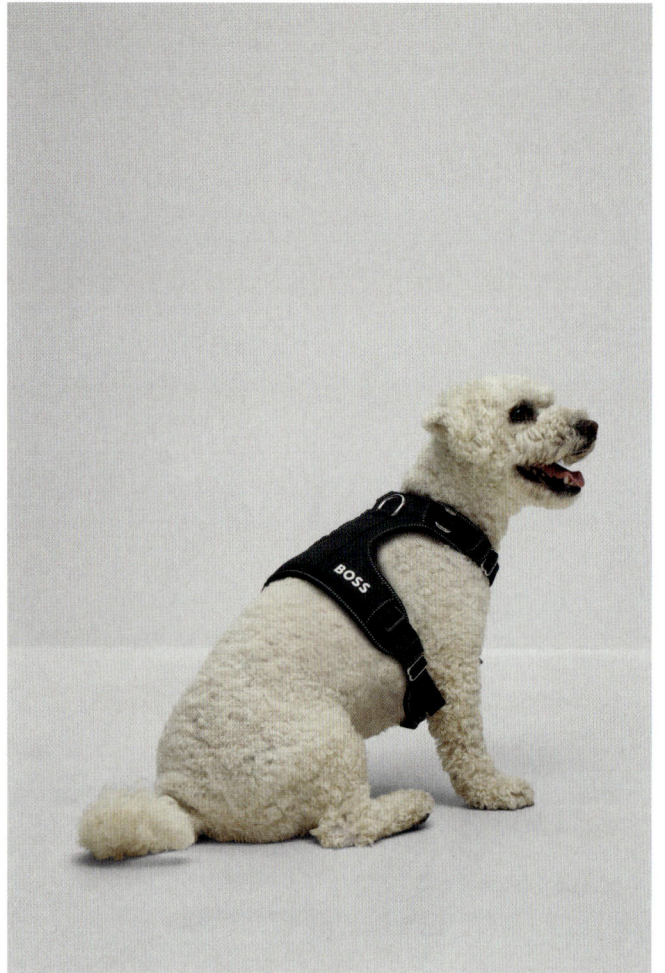

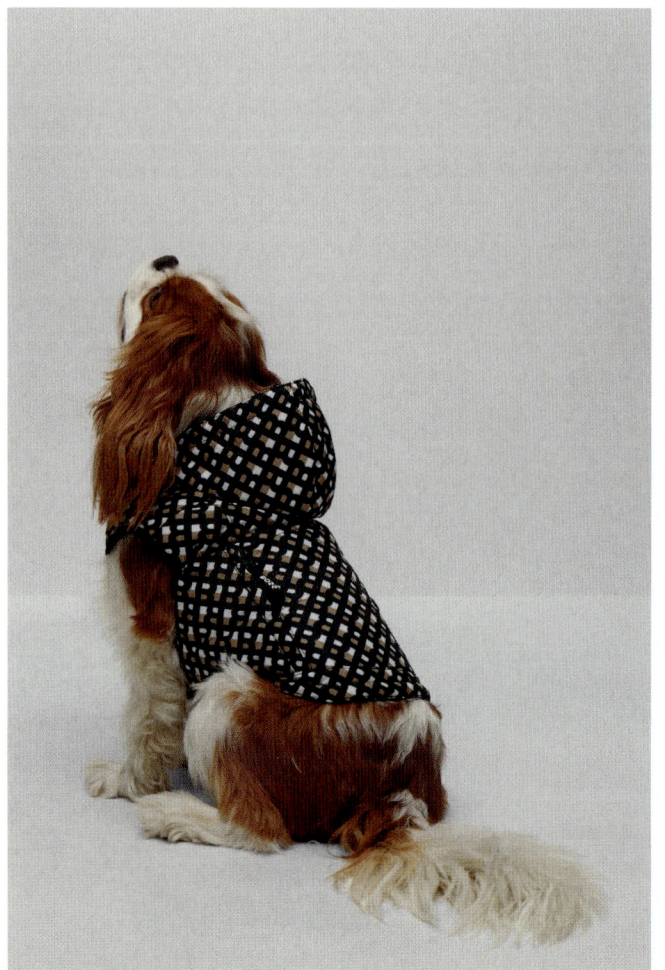

Four-legged in vogue
Vierbeiner in Mode

Luxury brands have not forgotten about human's best, four-legged, friends and have created versatile collections of accessories, clothes, and toys, like the one for dogs from BOSS. Kept in the brand's signature palette of colours, it offers a wide range of high-end products.

Auch die besten, vierbeinigen, Freunde des Menschen werden von den Luxusmarken nicht vergessen, und so gibt es vielseitige Kollektionen von Accessoires, Kleidung und Spielzeug, wie jene für Hunde von BOSS. In der charakteristischen Farbpalette der Marke gehalten, bietet sie eine breite Palette von High-End-Produkten.

BOSS, DOG HARNESSES, DOG HOODIE WITH LOGO, DOG WATER-REPELLENT PADDED JACKET, DOG TRAVEL BAG WITH QUILTED MAT, DOG ROPE BALL TOY, DOG BALL SET
BOSS, HUNDE-GESCHIRRE, HUNDE-HOODIE MIT LOGO, WASSERABWEISENDE, WATTIERTE HUNDEJACKE, HUNDE-REISETASCHE MIT GESTEPPTER MATTE, HUNDE-SEILSPIELZEUG, HUNDEBÄLLE IM SET

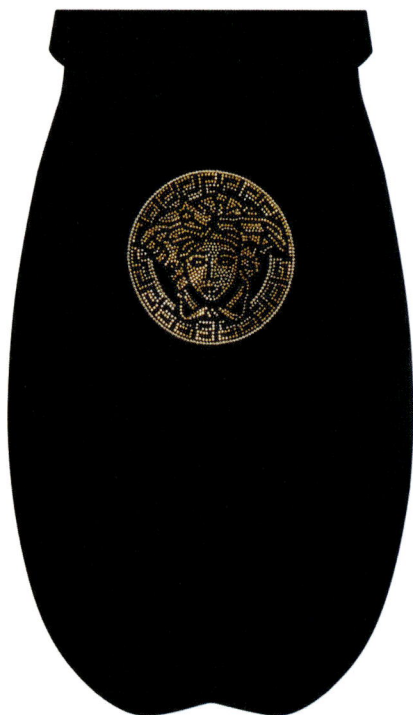

The quintessence of elegance, Versace infuses its pet accessories collection with luxury materials and designs. The dog collar and harness are stylishly decorated, refined pieces of clothing embellished with iconic motifs of Medusa, as are the accessories, including a comfortable bed in the typical Baroque pattern.

Versace steht für die Quintessenz von Eleganz und verwendet für die Haustier-Kollektion luxuriöse Materialien und Designs. Hundehalsband und -geschirr sind stilvoll dekoriert und die edlen Kleidungsstücke mit dem ikonischen Medusa-Motiv verziert, ebenso wie die Accessoires, darunter ein bequemes Bett mit dem typischen Barockmuster.

VERSACE, I LOVE BAROQUE SMALL PET BED, I LOVE BAROQUE LARGE PET BED

<VERSACE, CRYSTAL ICON PET COLLAR, ICON PET COLLAR, ICON PET LEASH, ICON PET HARNESS, CRYSTAL MEDUSA PET RAINCOAT

VERSACE, HAUSTIERBETT I LOVE BAROQUE KLEIN, HAUSTIERBETT I LOVE BAROQUE GROSS

<

VERSACE, HAUSTIER-HALSBAND CRYSTAL ICON, HAUSTIER-HALSBAND ICON, LEINE ICON FÜR HAUSTIERE, GESCHIRR ICON, REGENMANTEL CRYSTAL MEDUSA FÜR HAUSTIERE

GUCCI, SMALL GG PET
CARRIER WITH WEB,
PET HARNESS, PET
GG COAT, PET WOOL
BLEND SWEATER WITH
INTERLOCKING G
GUCCI, TRAGETASCHE
FÜR KLEINE HAUSTIERE
MIT GG UND WEB,
GESCHIRR FÜR
HAUSTIERE, GG
HAUSTIERMANTEL,
HAUSTIERPULLOVER AUS
WOLLMISCHUNG MIT GG

The distinctive pet carrier from Gucci
is a comfortable and easy-to-carry bag,
enriched with the brand's logo and signature
materials – GG Supreme canvas in beige
and blue. The Harness from the Gucci Love
Parade collection also celebrates the House's
emblematic green and red web stripes
and is made from sustainable materials.
The elegant coat reinvents the historic
GG Supreme canvas in a beige and ebony
colour version with a tonal trim.
The interlocking G pattern also
covers the cosy wool blend sweater.

Die unverwechselbare Haustiertasche
von Gucci ist eine bequeme und leicht zu
tragende Tasche, die mit dem Logo der
Marke und den typischen Stoffen –
GG-Supreme-Canvas in Beige und Blau –
ausstaffiert ist. Das Geschirr aus der Gucci
Love-Parade-Kollektion zelebriert ebenfalls
die emblematischen grünen und roten
Webstreifen des Hauses und besteht
aus nachhaltigen Materialien.
Der elegante Mantel erfindet den
historischen GG-Supreme-Canvas in einer
beige- und ebenholzfarbenen Version
mit farblich abgestimmtem Besatz neu.
Das Muster mit den ineinandergreifenden
Gs bedeckt auch den kuscheligen Pullover
aus einer Wollmischung.

sieger design has envisioned an elegant cat
feeding station with high-quality porcelain
bowls for the brand LucyBalu. The thoughtful
positioning of the handle on the tray ensures
that it can be carried without moving
the bowls. The set also consists of a slow
feeder with a relief pattern and a cloche
to cover the food.

sieger design hat für die Marke LucyBalu
eine elegante Katzenfutterstation mit
hochwertigen Porzellannäpfen entworfen.
Durch den gut positionierten Griff kann
das Tablett getragen werden, ohne dass
die Schalen verrutschen. Das Set umfasst
des Weiteren einen Slow Feeder mit
Reliefmuster und eine Glocke zum
Abdecken des Futters.

SIEGER BY FÜRSTENBERG, LUCYBALU, MICHAEL SIEGER WITH CAT LUNA
SIEGER BY FÜRSTENBERG, LUCYBALU, MICHAEL SIEGER MIT KATZE LUNA

Prada designed a diverse collection of accessories and clothes for dogs made of nylon, which is a fabric that was first introduced to the luxury world by Prada and, as the brand emphasises, is an important part of its genetic code.

Aus dem Hause Prada stammt eine vielfältige Kollektion von Accessoires und Kleidung aus Nylon für Hunde. Das Material, das ursprünglich von Prada in die Luxuswelt eingeführt wurde, ist, wie die Marke betont, ein wichtiger Teil der Unternehmens-DNA.

PRADA, RE-NYLON DOG HARNESS, RE-NYLON DOG RAINCOAT WITH HOOD, COTTON FLEECE HOODIE FOR PETS
PRADA, HUNDEGESCHIRR AUS RE-NYLON, HUNDEREGENMANTEL AUS RE-NYLON MIT KAPUZE, KAPUZENPULLOVER AUS BAUMWOLLFLEECE FÜR HAUSTIERE

To keep dogs warm, Prada has envisioned
a series of sweaters in a blend of wool
and cashmere that have been inspired by
designs from its menswear and womenswear
collections. The high-quality garments
are decorated with the iconic intarsia
lettering logo.

Um Hunde warmzuhalten, hat Prada eine
Reihe von Pullovern aus einer Mischung
aus Wolle und Kaschmir entworfen,
die von Designs aus den Herren- und
Damenkollektionen inspiriert wurden.
Die hochwertigen Kleidungsstücke sind
mit dem ikonischen Intarsien-
Buchstabenlogo verziert.

PRADA, WOOL AND CASHMERE DOG SWEATERS
PRADA, HUNDEPULLOVER AUS WOLLE UND
KASCHMIR

PRADA, CRYSTAL-STUDDED SATIN DOG HARNESS, CRYSTAL-STUDDED SATIN PET COLLAR, RE-NYLON PET LEASH
PRADA, HUNDEGESCHIRR AUS KRISTALLBESETZTEM SATIN, HAUSTIERHALSBAND AUS KRISTALLBESETZTEM SATIN, HAUSTIERLEINE AUS RE-NYLON

The harness and collar are made of satin that has been embellished with all-over (artificial) crystals that create a sophisticated and precious look. The final touch is the iconic enamelled metal triangle logo, which first appeared on trunks designed by Mario Prada in 1913.

Das Satin-Geschirr und das Halsband sind über und über mit (unechten) Kristallen verziert, was einen edlen, kostspieligen Look ergibt. Für den letzten Schliff sorgt das ikonische Dreieckslogo aus emailliertem Metall, das erstmals 1913 auf den von Mario Prada entworfenen Koffern zu sehen war.

DIOR, PET HARNESS AND LEASH, HIT THE ROAD TRANSPORTATION BAG
DIOR, GESCHIRR UND LEINE FÜR HAUSTIERE, TRAGETASCHE HIT THE ROAD

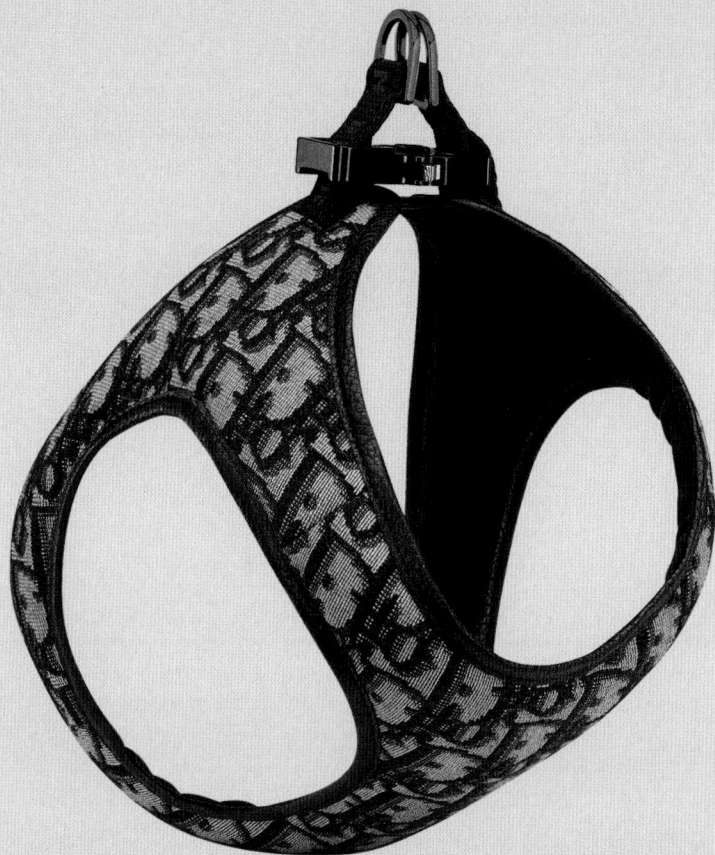

One of the novelties in the Dior collection for pets is the refined Hit the Road carrying bag with a large zip opening to access a spacious compartment and one side made of Cannage Cosmos leather for optimal breathability, as well as handles and an adjustable shoulder strap. The leash and harness are crafted using Nylon Jacquard with the Dior signature.

Eine Neuheit in Diors Kollektion für Haustiere ist die elegante Hit-the-Road-Tragetasche mit einer großen Reißverschlussöffnung ins geräumige Innere, Cannage-Cosmos-Leder auf einer Seite für optimale Atmungsaktivität, sowie Tragegriffen und einem verstellbaren Schultergurt. Leine und Geschirr sind aus Nylon-Jacquard mit dem Dior-Schriftzug gefertigt.

PAGERIE, THE BABBI
PAGERIE, GESCHIRR THE BABBI

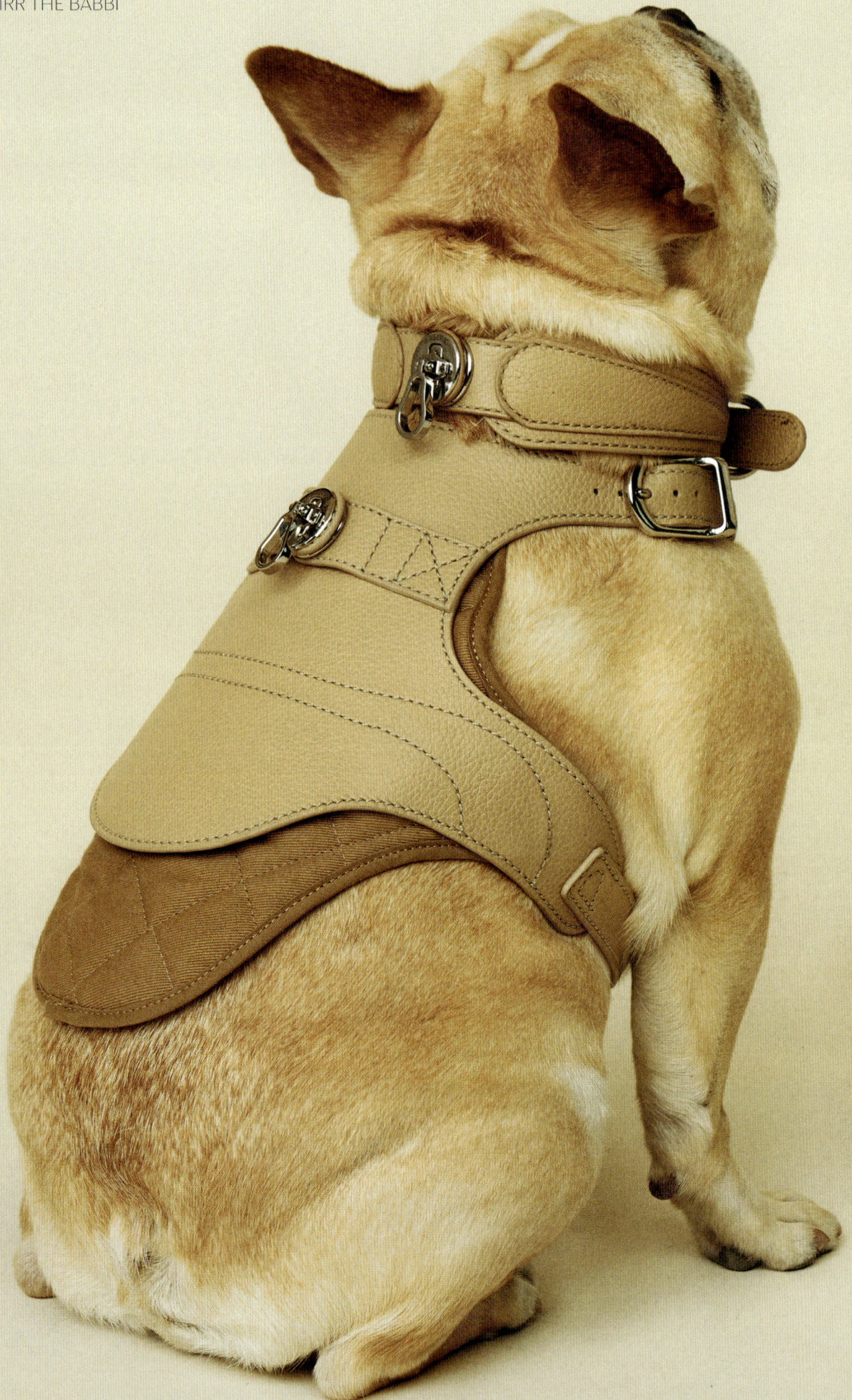

PAGERIE, THE SIMONE
PAGERIE, GESCHIRR THE SIMONE

PAGERIE, THE GALE
PAGERIE, HUNDELEINE THE GALE

Focusing on the highest quality products
for pets, PAGERIE holds craftsmanship and
sustainability at the heart of every design.
The large collection of luxury leashes, collars,
and harnesses is complete with practical
accessories like a luxurious blanket and
a deluxe grooming set, but also offers objects
for pets' owners, including the Margot
Whistle for training pets or grabbing
their attention.

PAGERIE konzentriert sich auf Produkte
von höchster Qualität für Haustiere und
stellt Handwerkskunst und Nachhaltigkeit
in den Mittelpunkt jedes Designs. Die große
Kollektion an Luxusleinen, Halsbändern und
Geschirren wird ergänzt durch praktisches
Zubehör wie eine hochwertige Decke und
ein luxuriöses Pflegeset, bietet aber auch
Gegenstände für Herrchen und Frauchen,
darunter die Hundepfeife The Margot,
mit der der Vierbeiner erzogen oder zur
Aufmerksamkeit gemahnt werden kann.

PAGERIE, THE PANSAGE SET, THE MARGOT,
THE MAZONE BLANKET
PAGERIE, PFLEGESET THE PANSAGE,
PFEIFE THE MARGOT, DECKE THE MAZONE

HOME
ZUHAUSE

Cheers!
Prost!

A highly curated lifestyle starts at home, where some exceptional objects turn everyday activities into a luxury experience. To start with raising a glass to the refined tools for living around us – the James Shaker and Thomas Wine Set, including a bottle opener, pour spout, and cap, from Louis Vuitton features the signature Damoflage pattern from Pharrell Williams' debut Men's show. The golden finish gives them both some added glamour.

Ein außergewöhnlicher Lebensstil beginnt in den eigenen vier Wänden, wo ein paar ausgefallene Objekte alltägliche Aktivitäten in eine exklusive Erfahrung verwandeln. Also heben wir das Glas auf die veredelten Alltagsgegenstände um uns herum – Louis Vuittons Mixbecher James und das Wein-Set Thomas, das einen Flaschenöffner, einen Ausgießer und einen Verschlusskorken beinhaltet, sind beide mit dem charakteristischen Damoflage-Motiv aus Pharrell Williams' erster Herrenshow verziert. Das goldene Finish verleiht beiden zusätzlichen Glamour.

LOUIS VUITTON, JAMES SHAKER GOLD
AND THOMAS WINE SET GOLD
LOUIS VUITTON, MIXBECHER JAMES
GOLD UND WEIN-SET THOMAS GOLD

For his corkscrew Marcel Wanders selects
a jester in a colourful diamond costume –
opening a bottle sets him in motion,
with stretching movements that refer
to a jester's typical dances and jumps.
The Circus collection by the designer
also includes a one-of-a-kind nutcracker
employing the strongman character –
perfect for the task.

Für seinen Korkenzieher wählt Marcel
Wanders einen Narren im bunten
Rautenkostüm – das Öffnen der Flasche
erinnert an die typischen Streck- und
Sprungbewegungen eines Narrentanzes.
Zur Circus-Kollektion des Designers gehört
auch ein einzigartiger Nussknacker in Form
eines Kraftmenschen – wie geschaffen
für diese Aufgabe.

ALESSI, THE JESTER CORKSCREW AND STRONGMAN
NUTCRACKER BY MARCEL WANDERS
ALESSI, KORKENZIEHER THE JESTER UND NUSSKNACKER
STRONGMAN VON MARCEL WANDERS

Artfully crafted from porcelain, these elegant and original champagne coolers have a striking sculptural quality, whether as a reference to an exotic mask or the diamond cushion pattern. The best company would be the radiant Sip of Gold champagne tumblers with a 24-carat gold finish on the inside – a pleasant blend of luxury and artistry.

Kunstvoll aus Porzellan gefertigt, haben diese eleganten und originellen Champagnerkühler eine auffallende skulpturale Qualität, sowohl in der Form einer exotischen Maske als auch im Kissenrelief mit Rautenmuster. Die beste Gesellschaft sind gewiss die strahlenden Champagnerbecher Sip of Gold mit einem 24-Karat-Goldfinish auf der Innenseite – eine wunderbare Mischung von Luxus und Kunstfertigkeit.

SIEGER BY FÜRSTENBERG,
SIP OF GOLD CHAMPAGNE TUMBLERS
SIEGER BY FÜRSTENBERG,
CHAMPAGNERBECHER SIP OF GOLD

SIEGER BY FÜRSTENBERG, FACES
AND CUSHION CHAMPAGNE COOLERS
SIEGER BY FÜRSTENBERG,
CHAMPAGNERKÜHLER FACES
UND CUSHION

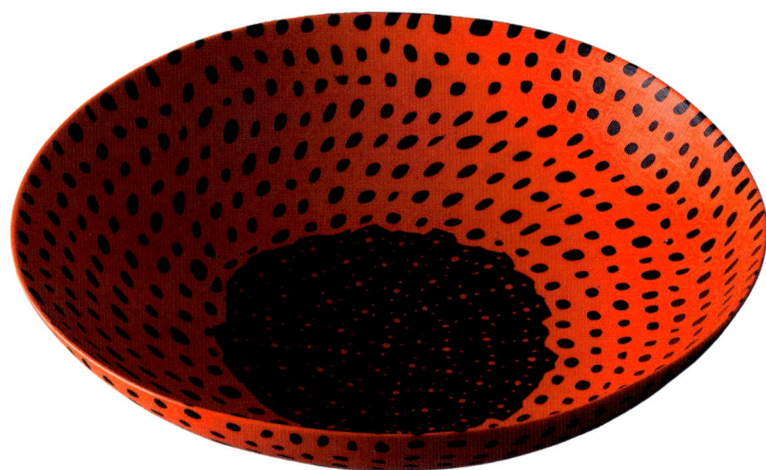

VENINI, MURRINE OPACHE
COLLECTION BY CARLO SCARPA
VENINI, KOLLEKTION MURRINE
OPACHE VON CARLO SCARPA

SIEGER BY FÜRSTENBERG,
"MY CHINA!" BREAD BASKET
SIEGER BY FÜRSTENBERG,
BROTKORB „MY CHINA!"

ZAHA HADID DESIGN,
SWIRL BOWL IN MARBLE
ZAHA HADID DESIGN, SCHALE
SWIRL AUS MARMOR

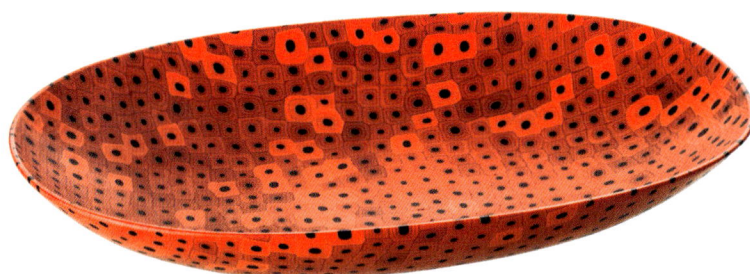

This is a bowl
Dies ist eine Schale

In his collection of black and coral bowls, Carlo Scarpa demonstrates the refinement of Murano techniques and gives the glassware the highest prestige.
"MY CHINA!", part of a multifunctional dinner service, this sculptural yet minimalist porcelain bread basket will be a perfect addition to modern table decor.
Zaha Hadid Design, following the architect's heritage, tends to design objects that are dynamic and surprising but also informed by the organic world, which the Swirl Bowl exemplifies.

In seiner Kollektion schwarzer und korallenroter Schalen demonstriert Carlo Scarpa die Verfeinerung der Murano-Techniken und erschafft auf diese Weise Glaswaren von höchster Qualität.
„MY CHINA!": Als Teil eines multi-funktionalen Tafelservices ist dieser skulpturale und zugleich minimalistische Brotkorb aus Porzellan eine perfekte Ergänzung für die moderne Tischdekoration.
Zaha Hadid Design folgt dem Erbe der Architektin und überrascht immer wieder mit dynamischen, von organischen Formen inspirierten Objekten, wie die Schale Swirl veranschaulicht.

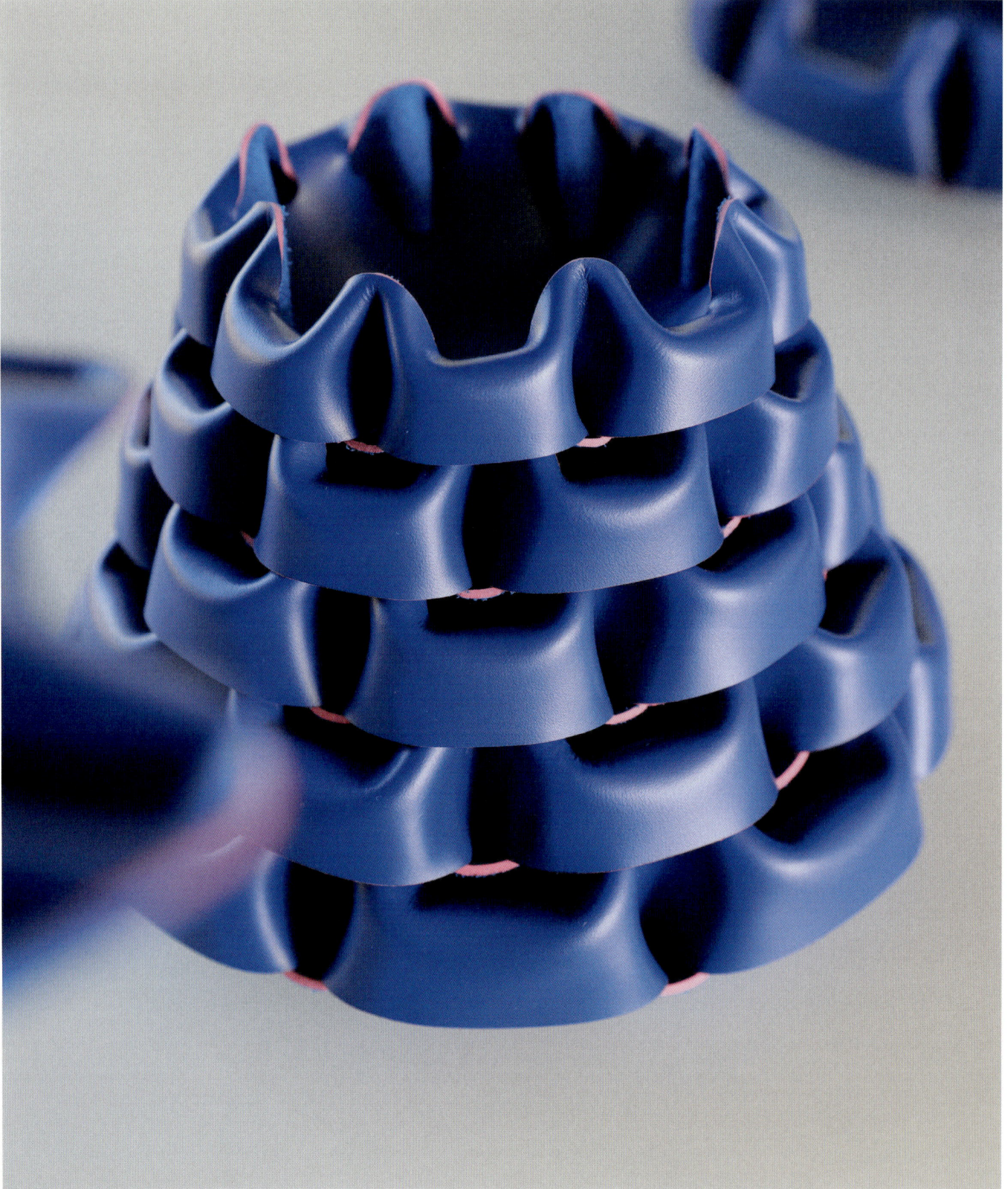

For Louis Vuitton's Objets Nomades
collection, Atelier Oï and Patricia Urquiola
designed the most extraordinary bowls
made of the highest quality leather.
The refined folds of the material
create surprising shapes, enhanced by
sophisticated and distinctive colour
palette. Essentially beautiful, the objects
are perfectly functional.

Für die Kollektion Objets Nomades von
Louis Vuitton entwarfen Atelier Oï und
Patricia Urquiola die außergewöhnlichsten
Schalen aus hochwertigem Leder.
Die Raffung des Materials kreiert
überraschende Formen, die durch eine
wohldurchdachte, unverwechselbare
Farbpalette unterstrichen werden.
Die Objekte sind nicht nur ausgesprochen
schön, sondern erfüllen darüber hinaus
auf perfekte Weise ihre Funktion.

LOUIS VUITTON, ORIGAMI BOWLS BY ATELIER OÏ
AND OVERLAY BOWL BY PATRICIA URQUIOLA
LOUIS VUITTON, ORIGAMI-SCHALEN VON
ATELIER OÏ UND OVERLAY BOWL VON PATRICIA
URQUIOLA

A piece of cake
Etwas Süßes

The Fatman sparkles with colours when folded up – once open it offers three large plates to serve cakes. The structure can be easily carried thanks to the head-handle. Baccarat offers a more classic pastry stand that masterly features the beauty and elegance of crystal. The Seal and Off The Moon stands, from maximalism to simple lines, translate functionality into highly elaborated decoration.

Zusammengeklappt erstrahlt der Fatman farbenfroh in seiner ganzen Pracht – einmal geöffnet wird er zur Etagere mit drei großen Serviertellern für Gebäck. Dank des Kopfteils, der zum Griff wird, kann das Gestell gut getragen werden. Von Baccarat stammt eine klassischere Gebäcketagere, in der die Schönheit und Eleganz von Kristall meisterhaft zum Ausdruck kommt. Der überbordende Ständer The Seal und das schlicht gehaltene Tablett Off The Moon, übersetzen auf je eigene Weise Funktionalität in perfekt durchdachte Raumdekoration.

CAPPELLINI, OFF THE MOON TRAY
BY THOMAS DARIEL
CAPPELLINI, TABLETT OFF THE
MOON VON THOMAS DARIEL

<
ALESSI, FATMAN, FOLDING CAKE
STAND AND THE SEAL STAND
BY MARCEL WANDERS
ALESSI, FALTBARE ETAGERE FATMAN
UND KUCHENSTÄNDER THE SEAL
VON MARCEL WANDERS

BACCARAT, MILLE NUITS
SMALL PASTRY STAND
BACCARAT, KLEINER
GEBÄCKSTÄNDER MILLE NUITS

ALESSI, LA CONICA MANICO
LUNGO,
ESPRESSO COFFEE MAKER
BY ALDO ROSSI
ALESSI, ESPRESSOKOCHER LA
CONICA MANICO LUNGO VON
ALDO ROSSI

>
BACCARAT X ALESSI, HARCOURT
ESPRESSO FOR TWO
BACCARAT X ALESSI, HARCOURT
ESPRESSO FOR TWO

Coffee or tea?
Kaffee oder Tee?

There are very many coffee makers and tea sets, but only a few can give the ritual of drinking a touch of chic. Aldo Rossi's sophisticated play of elegant volumes has become iconic. Alessi also collaborated with Baccarat to create a stylish set for two with perfectly shaped crystal cups accompanying a Moka coffee maker.

Es gibt sehr viele Kaffeemaschinen und Tee-Sets, aber nur wenige verleihen dem Ritual des Trinkens einen Hauch von Chic. Aldo Rossis raffiniertes Spiel mit eleganten Volumina ist mittlerweile ikonisch. Alessi hat darüber hinaus mit Baccarat zusammengearbeitet und ein stilvolles Set für zwei Personen kreiert, das aus perfekt geformten Kristallbechern und einer Espressokanne besteht.

Baccarat designed an equally sleek set for drinking tea with a nice contrast between the crystal glasses and porcelain tea pot. Prada's refined charm is in the pleasant shape of its tea cups, highlighted by an iconic checkerboard pattern. For all aficionados of the ultra-modern DATUM, the first porcelain series designed by the acclaimed architectural studio Foster + Partners for FÜRSTENBERG features delightful geometric forms and interesting proportions.

Von Baccarat stammt ein ebenso elegantes Tee-Set, mit einem schönen Kontrast zwischen den Kristallgläsern und der Porzellanteekanne. Pradas kultivierter Charme zeigt sich in der schmeichelnden Form der Teetassen, die durch das legendäre Schachbrettmuster hervorgehoben wird. Den Fans der ultramodernen Porzellanserie DATUM, die vom renommierten Architekturbüro Foster + Partners für FÜRSTENBERG entworfen wurde, werden reizvolle geometrische Formen und interessante Proportionen geboten.

BACCARAT, HARCOURT FAUNACRYSTOPOLIS TEA SET
BACCARAT, FAUNACRYSTOPOLIS HARCOURT TEE-SET

PRADA, SET OF TWO PORCELAIN TEA CUPS – CHECKERBOARD
PRADA, SET MIT ZWEI TEETASSEN AUS PORZELLAN – CHECKERBOARD

>

PORZELLANMANUFAKTUR FÜRSTENBERG, DATUM BY FOSTER + PARTNERS
PORZELLANMANUFAKTUR FÜRSTENBERG, DATUM VON FOSTER + PARTNERS

VERSACE ROSENTHAL, JUNGLE ANIMALIER COFFEE CUP AND
SAUCER SET
VERSACE ROSENTHAL, JUNGLE ANIMALIER, KAFFEETASSEN UND
–UNTERTASSEN

>
VERSACE ROSENTHAL, VERSACE MEDUSA RHAPSODY TEA SET
VERSACE ROSENTHAL, VERSACE TEESERVICE MEDUSA RHAPSODY

The Medusa Rhapsody Tea Set, adorned with
the enriching motif of Barocco flowers, sets yet
another atmosphere for a tea drinking routine, just
like the attractively packed and lavishly decorated
sets of espresso cups with saucers that effortlessly
combine Versace's stylish luxury with Rosenthal's
highest quality porcelain.

Das Teeservice Medusa Rhapsody,
geschmückt mit dem überbordenden
Barocco-Motiv, inspiriert auf ganz eigene
Art zum regelmäßigen Teetrinken, ebenso
wie die hübsch verpackten und aufwendig
dekorierten Sets von Espressotassen
und -untertassen, die ganz mühelos
Versaces luxuriöse Eleganz mit Rosenthals
hochwertigem Porzellan verbinden.

The collection of 30 mugs with lids
celebrating 30 years of artistic collaboration
between Versace and Rosenthal gathers
iconic designs, each one unique. The cups
can be bought individually or in a precious
set, striking in its variety and visually
powerful patterns.

Die Kollektion von 30 Bechern mit
Deckel feiert 30 Jahre der künstlerischen
Zusammenarbeit zwischen Versace und
Rosenthal und versammelt einzigartige,
ikonische Designs. Die Tassen können
einzeln oder in einem edlen Set gekauft
werden, das durch seine Vielfalt und
aussagekräftigen Muster besticht.

VERSACE ROSENTHAL, 30 YEARS MUG COLLECTION
VERSACE ROSENTHAL, BECHERSAMMLUNG 30 JAHRE

Arts de la table at its best, this rich Caribe
porcelain collection is a feast for the eyes
and an extraordinary way to celebrate meals.
A true explosion of colour, it becomes
a canvas for joyous scenes of fantastic
animals and abundant nature, with a final
gold and platinum touch.

Arts de la table von seiner besten Seite:
die üppige Porzellanserie Caribe ist eine
Augenweide und eine außergewöhnliche
Art, Mahlzeiten zu zelebrieren. Mit einer
wahren Farbexplosion wird das Geschirr
zur Leinwand für fröhliche Szenen voller
fantastischer Tiere und wilder Natur,
abgerundet durch einen Hauch
von Gold und Platin.

CHRISTIAN LACROIX FOR VISTA
ALEGRE, CARIBE COLLECTION
CHRISTIAN LACROIX FÜR VISTA
ALEGRE, CARIBE COLLECTION

A meeting of luxury, beauty, and craftsmanship
– Baccarat invites us to fill every day with joyful
festivities. The large collection of crystal glasses
for all occasions features delightful, sophisticated
shapes, with a particular spotlight on the sublime
crystal in vivid colours.

Ein Zusammentreffen von Luxus, Schönheit
und Handwerkskunst – Baccarat lädt uns ein,
jeden Tag mit fröhlicher Festlichkeit zu füllen.
Die große Sammlung von Kristallgläsern
für alle Gelegenheiten zeichnet sich durch
reizvolle, raffinierte Formen aus, wobei
fraglos der Fokus auf dem edlen Kristall
in leuchtenden Farben liegt.

BACCARAT, MILLE NUITS FLUTISSIMO FLUTES,
HARMONIE COLORS OF JOY TUMBLERS SET

BACCARAT, SEKTFLÖTEN MILLE NUITS FLUTISSIMO,
TRINKBECHER-SET HARMONIE COLORS OF JOY

>
BACCARAT, HARCOURT 1841 GLASS
BACCARAT, GLAS HARCOURT 1841

Haute Couture kitchen
Haute Couture Küche

For all who would like to invite haute couture into their kitchens, the collaboration between Christian Lacroix and Maison Schmid, a French manufacturer specialising in kitchen design, will certainly be interesting. The modern furniture is stylised with fashionable patterns, which can entirely transform a kitchen's atmosphere.

Für alle, die Haute Couture in ihre Küche bringen möchten, wird die Zusammenarbeit zwischen Christian Lacroix und Maison Schmidt, einem französischen Unternehmen, das sich auf Küchendesign spezialisiert hat, sicherlich interessant sein. Die modernen Möbel tragen modische Muster, die die Atmosphäre einer Küche völlig verändern können.

CHRISTIAN LACROIX MAISON FOR MAISON SCHMIDT.
PRÊTE-MOI TA PLUME AND ALGAE BLOOM COLLECTIONS
CHRISTIAN LACROIX MAISON FÜR MAISON SCHMIDT.
PRÊTE-MOI TA PLUME UND ALGAE BLOOM COLLECTIONS

VERSACE, MEDUSA CUTLERY, CRETE DE FLEUR APRON KITCHEN SET
VERSACE, BESTECK MEDUSA, KÜCHENSCHÜRZEN-SET CRETE
DE FLEUR

ALESSI, OCCASIONAL OBJECT CUTLERY SET BY VIRGIL ABLOH
ALESSI, BESTECKSET OCCASIONAL OBJECT VON VIRGIL ABLOH

The art of cooking depends not only
on the recipes and ingredients but also on
the tools we use in the kitchen, from a kettle
for preparing tea to a strainer. Envisioned
by leading designers or acclaimed architects,
these objects add a pinch of fantasy
to kitchen spaces through their original
forms – an ideal choice for a luxury,
open-plan kitchen.

Kochkunst hängt nicht nur von den
Rezepten und Zutaten ab, sondern auch
von den Werkzeugen, die wir in der
Küche verwenden, vom Wasserkocher
für die Zubereitung von Tee bis zum
Sieb. Von führenden Designerinnen oder
renommierten Architekten entworfen,
verleihen diese Objekte Küchenräumen
durch ihre originellen Formen einen Hauch
von Fantasie – die ideale Wahl für eine
luxuriöse, offene Küche.

ALESSI, CONVIVIO BY DAVID CHIPPERFIELD,
ALESSI, CONVIVIO VON DAVID CHIPPERFIELD

ALESSI, MAX LE CHINOS BY PHILIPPE STARCK
< PITO KETTLE BY FRANK GEHRY
STANDSIEB MAX LE CHINOIS VON PHILIPPE STARCK
< WASSERKESSEL PITO VON FRANK GEHRY

179

Inspired by the sun
Von der Sonne inspiriert

The collaboration between Dolce & Gabbana and Smeg (with design by Matteo Bazzicalupo and Raffaella Mangiarotti) brought about two exceptional collections of kitchen appliances, adorned with lavish patterns that are manufactured through an artistic decoration reproduction process that is based on an initial hand-painted prototype. Blu Mediterraneo pays tribute to the colours of the sea and the sky, while Sicily is my Love highlights a vivid palette of red, orange, and yellow, identified with the island's traditions. The patterns of both series work perfectly with the retro-inspired, rounded shapes of Smeg's toasters, juicers, kettles, mixers, and much more.

Die Zusammenarbeit zwischen Dolce & Gabbana und Smeg (entworfen von Matteo Bazzicalupo und Raffaella Mangiarotti) brachte zwei außergewöhnliche Kollektionen von aufwendig verzierten Küchengeräten hervor, die in einem künstlerischen Dekorationsverfahren hergestellt werden, das auf einem ersten handbemalten Prototyp basiert. Blu Mediterraneo ist eine Hommage an die Farben des Meeres und des Himmels, während Sicily is my Love den Fokus auf eine lebhafte Farbpalette aus Rot, Orange und Gelb legt, die mit den Traditionen der Insel identifiziert wird. Die Designs beider Serien passen perfekt zu den retro-inspirierten, abgerundeten Formen der Toaster, Entsafter, Wasserkocher, Mixer und vielem mehr von Smeg.

SMEG X DOLCE & GABBANA, BLU MEDITERRANEO AND SICILY IS MY LOVE
SMEG X DOLCE & GABBANA, BLU MEDITERRANEO UND SICILY IS MY LOVE

CHRISTIAN LACROIX MAISON FOR DESIGNERS GUILD, CUSHIONS DAME NATURE, LE CURIEUX, JARDIN DES HESPÉRIDES AND ARLECCHINO WOOD
CHRISTIAN LACROIX FÜR DESIGNERS GUILD, KISSEN DAME NATURE, LE CURIEUX, JARDIN DES HESPÉRIDES UND ARLECCHINO WOOD

>

CHRISTIAN LACROIX MAISON FOR DESIGNERS GUILD, CUSHION LACROIX PARADISE BY PHILIPPE GARCIA
CHRISTIAN LACROIX MAISON FÜR DESIGNERS GUILD, KISSEN LACROIX PARADISE VON PHILIPPE GARCIA

Powerful patterns
Kraftvolle Muster

Proof of how expressive patterns can be is in the pillow and blanket collections of luxury brands. Christian Lacroix's universe is filled with imaginative motifs, often inspired by the natural world or drawing from artistic creations. The ornamental decorations are often based on intriguing collages and vibrant with colours.

Wie ausdrucksstark Muster wirken können, zeigen die Kissen- und Deckenkollektionen von Luxusmarken sehr eindrücklich. Das Universum von Christian Lacroix ist erfüllt von fantasievollen Motiven, die häufig von der Natur oder von künstlerischen Kreationen inspiriert sind. Die reich verzierten Objekte basieren oft auf faszinierenden Collagen und strotzen vor Farben.

FENDI CASA, KARL 2 CUSHION,
BIG KARL PLAID
FENDI CASA, KISSEN KARL 2, PLAID
BIG KARL

GUCCI, HORSEBIT COTTON
JACQUARD CUSHION
GUCCI, KISSEN AUS
BAUMWOLLJACQUARD
MIT HORSEBIT-MUSTER

Other brands have focused purely on their
emblematic monograms. FENDI Casa's
designs celebrate the Karligraphy logo
designed by Karl Lagerfeld, which becomes
the all-over pattern of a velvet cushion and
a cosy blanket. Gucci draws the Horsebit
Jacquard with an equestrian element from
their archive. At Dior, the traditional Toile de
Jouy motif creates an elegant background for
the brand's logo.

Andere Marken haben sich ausschließlich
auf ihre emblematischen Monogramme
konzentriert. Die Designs von FENDI
Casa ehren das von Karl Lagerfeld
entworfene Karligraphy-Logo, das zum alles
bedeckenden Muster eines Samtkissens und
einer kuscheligen Decke wird. Gucci holt
mit dem Horsebit-Jacquard ein Reitsport-
Element aus seinem Archiv. Bei Dior bildet
das traditionelle Toile-de-Jouy-Motiv einen
eleganten Hintergrund für das Markenlogo.

DIOR, TOILE DE JOUY
SQUARE PILLOW TIGER
DIOR, QUADRATISCHES
KISSEN TOILE DE JOUY
MIT TIGER

For all enthusiasts of a more minimalist approach, the collection of pillows from Cassina creates a delightful optical illusion effect through geometric patterns and contrasting hues. The Kvadrat/Raf Simons pillows and blankets celebrate comfortable materials of the highest quality.

Für alle Fans eines minimalistischeren Ansatzes sorgt die Kissenkollektion von Cassina durch geometrische Muster und kontrastierende Farbtöne für reizvolle optische Täuschungen. Die Kissen und Decken von Kvadrat/Raf Simons setzen bequeme Materialien von höchster Qualität in Szene.

CASSINA, MIRROR FRAME CUSHIONS
CASSINA, KISSEN MIRROR FRAME

>
KVADRAT/RAF SIMONS, SHAKER SYSTEM PILLOWS AND BLANKETS
KVADRAT/RAF SIMONS, SHAKER SYSTEM KISSEN UND DECKEN

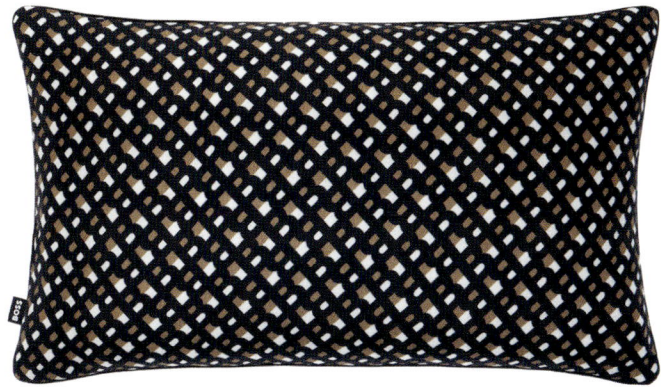

BOSS HOME, B MONOGRAM AND B LINEA BED LINEN,
PILLOWS WITH EMBROIDERED LOGO, KNITTED THROW
BOSS HOME, BETTWÄSCHE B MONOGRAM UND B LINEA,
KISSEN MIT LOGO-STICKEREI, GESTRICKTER ÜBERWURF

Seating arrangement
Sitzordnung

Luxury stands for quality, uniqueness, craftsmanship, artistry, and also for comfort. The organic shapes of the sofa and two armchairs, designed as part of the Objets Nomades collection by Louis Vuitton, offer an embracing experience. The Binda series envelops sitters with its sculptural and generous shape. Bulbo's petal elements are very soft, giving one the impression of being wrapped in a tropical flower.

Luxus steht für Qualität, Einzigartigkeit, Handwerk, Kunstfertigkeit und auch für Komfort. Die organischen Formen des Sofas und der zwei Sessel, die im Rahmen der Objets-Nomades-Kollektion von Louis Vuitton entworfen wurden, machen all dies erlebbar. Die Binda-Serie umarmt die Sitzenden mit ihrer skulpturalen, großzügigen Form. Bulbo vermittelt mit seinen weichen, blütenblattartigen Elementen das Gefühl, in eine tropische Blume gehüllt zu werden.

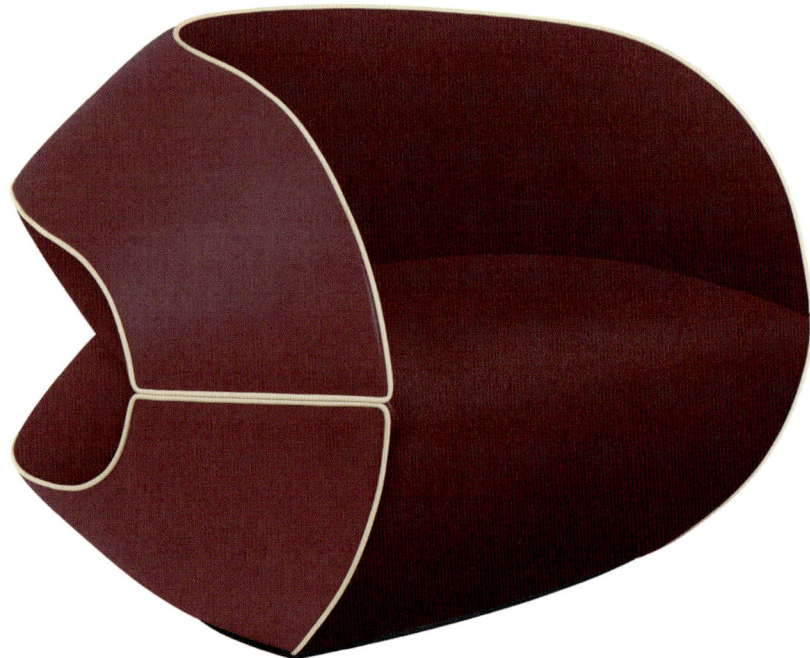

LOUIS VUITTON, BULBO ARMCHAIR
BY FERNANDO AND HUMBERTO
CAMPANA
LOUIS VUITTON, SESSEL BULBO
VON FERNANDO UND HUMBERTO
CAMPANA

<
LOUIS VUITTON, BINDA SOFA
AND ARMCHAIR BY RAW EDGES
LOUIS VUITTON, SOFA UND SESSEL
BINDA VON RAW EDGES

Sophistication with a dose of extravagance that adds an element of refreshing surprise to an interior – this could be the shortest definition of Cristina Celestino's The Happy Room collection for FENDI Casa. The refined materials, striking texture contrasts, and original colour palette make this collection even more distinctive.

Ein ausgereiftes Konzept mit einer Portion Extravaganz, die dem Interieur ein erfrischendes Überraschungselement verleiht – das ist vielleicht die kürzeste Definition von Cristina Celestinos Kollektion The Happy Room für FENDI Casa. Die feinen Stoffe, die auffälligen Materialkontraste und die originelle Farbpalette machen diese Kollektion noch unverwechselbarer.

FENDI CASA, THE HAPPY ROOM
COLLECTION BY CRISTINA CELESTINO
FENDI CASA, THE HAPPY ROOM,
KOLLEKTION VON CRISTINA CELESTINO

Between curves and folds, two stools also envisioned for the Objets Nomades family turn a home object considered insignificant into a small jewel. Blossom echoes Louis Vuitton's Monogram flowers, while Strap can become completely flat and carried as a small briefcase.

Mit Kurven und Kanten verwandeln zwei Hocker, die ebenfalls für die Serie Objets Nomades entworfen wurden, ein als unbedeutend angesehenes Wohnobjekt in ein kleines Juwel. Blossom erinnert an Louis Vuittons Monogrammblumen, während Strap komplett zusammengefaltet und als Ledermappe getragen werden kann.

LOUIS VUITTON, BLOSSOM STOOL BY TOKUJIN YOSHIOKA
LOUIS VUITTON, STUHL BLOSSOM VON TOKUJIN YOSHIOKA

>
LOUIS VUITTON, STOOL STRAP BY ATELIER OÏ
LOUIS VUITTON, HOCKER STRAP VON ATELIER OÏ

This iconic design by Virgil Abloh for
Cassina is a modular concept in the form
of characteristic black blocks, available in two
sizes, that can either stand alone or, when
combined, create a table or an ottoman.
The brand calls the project "an invitation
to play with one's imagination to create
new domestic landscapes and functions".
The structure comes in recycled wood
and the padding is partly derived from
biological sources.

Dieser ikonische Entwurf von Virgil Abloh für
Cassina ist ein modulares Konzept in Form
charakteristischer schwarzer Blöcke, die in
zwei Größen erhältlich sind und entweder
für sich stehen oder zusammengesteckt und
zum Tisch oder Polsterhocker umfunktioniert
werden können. Das Unternehmen
nennt das Projekt „eine Einladung, der
Fantasie freien Lauf zu lassen, um neue
Wohnlandschaften und -funktionen zu
kreieren". Das Gestell besteht aus recyceltem
Holz, der weiche Bezug aus PU mit einem
Anteil an pflanzlichen Polyolen.

CASSINA, MODULAR IMAGINATION BY VIRGIL ABLOH
CASSINA, MODULAR IMAGINATION VON VIRGIL ABLOH

CASSINA, TRAMONTO A NEW YORK SCREEN BY GAETANO PESCE
CASSINA, PARAVENT TRAMONTO A NEW YORK VON GAETANO PESCE

>

CASSINA, PARAVENTO BALLA BY GIACOMO BALLA
CASSINA, PARAVENTO BALLA VON GIACOMO BALLA

Movable walls
Bewegliche Wände

Privacy screens have the magical power to change the dynamic of a space, especially the most refined ones. Gaetano Pesce was inspired by the sunsets in New York and reconstructs the skyline of high-rises in coloured, semi-transparent polyurethane resin with a most sophisticated visual effect. Handcrafted, the screen is striking thanks to its sublime colour palette.
Another interesting room division is based on an original tempera and pencil sketch on paper by the Italian futurist artist Giacomo Balla. The elegant decorations are screen printed on both sides of wooden panels.

Sichtschutzwände können auf magische Weise die Dynamik eines Raums verändern, und das gilt insbesondere für die hochwertigsten Exemplare. Gaetano Pesce ließ sich von den Sonnenuntergängen in New York inspirieren und rekonstruiert die Skyline von Hochhäusern in farbigem, halbtransparentem Polyurethanharz, was zu beeindruckenden visuellen Effekten führt. Der handgefertigte Paravent fällt dank seiner erlesenen Farbpalette auf.
Ein weiterer interessanter Raumteiler basiert auf einer Originalskizze mit Tempera- und Bleistift auf Papier vom italienischen Futuristen Giacomo Balla. Die eleganten Farbflächen wurden beidseitig im Siebdruckverfahren auf Holzpaneele übertragen.

In The Happy Room collection, Cristina Celestino plays boldly with materials and combines them in original ways. For the two end panels of the screen, the designer invents a new material, "ETERE", obtained by treating fur with resin.

In der Kollektion The Happy Room spielt Cristina Celestino mutig mit Materialien und kombiniert sie auf originelle Weise. Für die beiden Enden des Wandschirms erfand die Designerin ein neues Material, „ETERE", das sie durch die Behandlung von Fell mit Harz erhält.

FENDI CASA, THE HAPPY ROOM SCREEN BY CRISTINA CELESTINO FENDI CASA, PARAVENT THE HAPPY ROOM VON CRISTINA CELESTINO

Creating atmosphere
Atmosphäre schaffen

Elegant candleholders can certainly help
to set the perfect mood for various spaces.
Whether intriguingly geometric, dynamically
organic, or tactile and sculptured, they can
create atmosphere while standing out as
a stylish highlight of any interior.

Elegante Kerzenhalter tragen sicherlich dazu
bei, die perfekte Stimmung in verschiedenen
Räumen zu schaffen. Ob faszinierend
geometrisch, dynamisch organisch oder
taktil und skulptural, sie rücken ein Zimmer
ins rechte Licht, und sind zugleich ein
stilvolles Highlight für jeden Innenraum.

CAPPELLINI, BLUE CANDLEHOLDERS
BY THOMAS DARIEL
CAPPELLINI, BLAUE KERZENHALTER
VON THOMAS DARIEL

GEORG JENSEN, COBRA FLOOR
CANDLEHOLDER
GEORG JENSEN, BODENKERZEN-
LEUCHTER COBRA

PP. 204–205 PORZELLAN MANUFAKTUR
NYMPHENBURG, "BERÜHRUNG"
BY ROLF SACHS
S. 204–205: PORZELLAN MANUFAKTUR
NYMPHENBURG, „BERÜHRUNG" VON
ROLF SACHS

ZAHA HADID DESIGN, CELL CANDLE HOLDER
ZAHA HADID DESIGN, KERZENHALTER CELL

VERSACE, MEDUSA TEA LIGHT HOLDER
VERSACE, TEELICHTHALTER MEDUSA

Versace has found the most inventive concept to embrace a common tea light – a simple yet sophisticated gesture. Available in three different colour finishes, they are all delicately embellished with the brand's iconic head of Medusa.

Den größten Einfallsreichtum zur Verschönerung eines gewöhnlichen Teelichts zeigt wohl Versace – ein schlichtes, aber absolut überzeugendes Design. Erhältlich in drei verschiedenen Farbausführungen, sind die Teelichthalter filigran mit dem ikonischen Medusenhaupt der Marke verziert.

Scented candles awaken yet another sense. Elegant porcelain versions with a lid, or more artistic elaborate glass models, will look chic in all spaces, from the living room to bathroom.

Duftkerzen wecken noch einen weiteren Sinn. Elegante Porzellanausführungen samt Deckel oder aufwändigere, künstlerische Modelle aus Glas sehen in allen Räumen schick aus, vom Wohnzimmer bis zum Badezimmer.

VERSACE ROSENTHAL, I LOVE BAROQUE AND VIRTUS GALA SCENTED CANDLES
VERSACE ROSENTHAL, DUFTKERZEN I LOVE BAROQUE UND VIRTUS GALA

PRADA, SCENTED CANDLES – CHECKER-BOARD, LIPSTICK STYLE, AND BANANA
PRADA, DUFTKERZEN – CHECKERBOARD, LIPSTICK UND BANANA

ZAHA HADID DESIGN, SHIMMER SCENTED CANDLE
ZAHA HADID DESIGN, DUFTKERZE SHIMMER

VENINI, VASE GRAN BULBO
BY PETER MARINO
VENINI, VASE GRAN BULBO
VON PETER MARINO

SIEGER BY FÜRSTENBERG,
LUNA COLLECTION
SIEGER BY FÜRSTENBERG,
KOLLEKTION LUNA

VENINI, GEODI VASE
BY SONIA PEDRAZZINI
VENINI, VASE GEODI
VON SONIA PEDRAZZINI

ALESSI, 100% MAKE-UP PROUST
VASE BY ALESSANDRO MENDINI
ALESSI, VASE 100% MAKE-UP
PROUST VON ALESSANDRO
MENDINI

It is difficult to imagine luxurious interiors without a sumptuous bouquet of flowers, and these need a proper vase for the total look. Be inspired by the refinement of Murano glass vases from Venini, the poetry of porcelain geometry of the Luna collection, or the state-of-art design by the master Alessandro Mendini inspired by Marcel Proust and the French pointillists.

Luxuriöse Innenräume sind ohne einen üppigen Blumenstrauß kaum vorstellbar, und für den vollständigen Look braucht es eine anständige Vase. Erfreuen Sie sich an den feinen Muranoglasvasen von Venini, der Porzellanpoesie der geometrischen Luna-Kollektion oder dem hochmodernen Design des Meisters Alessandro Mendini, der von Marcel Proust und den französischen Pointillisten inspiriert wurde.

CASSINA, SESTIERE BY PATRICIA URQUIOLA
CASSINA, SESTIERE VON PATRICIA URQUIOLA

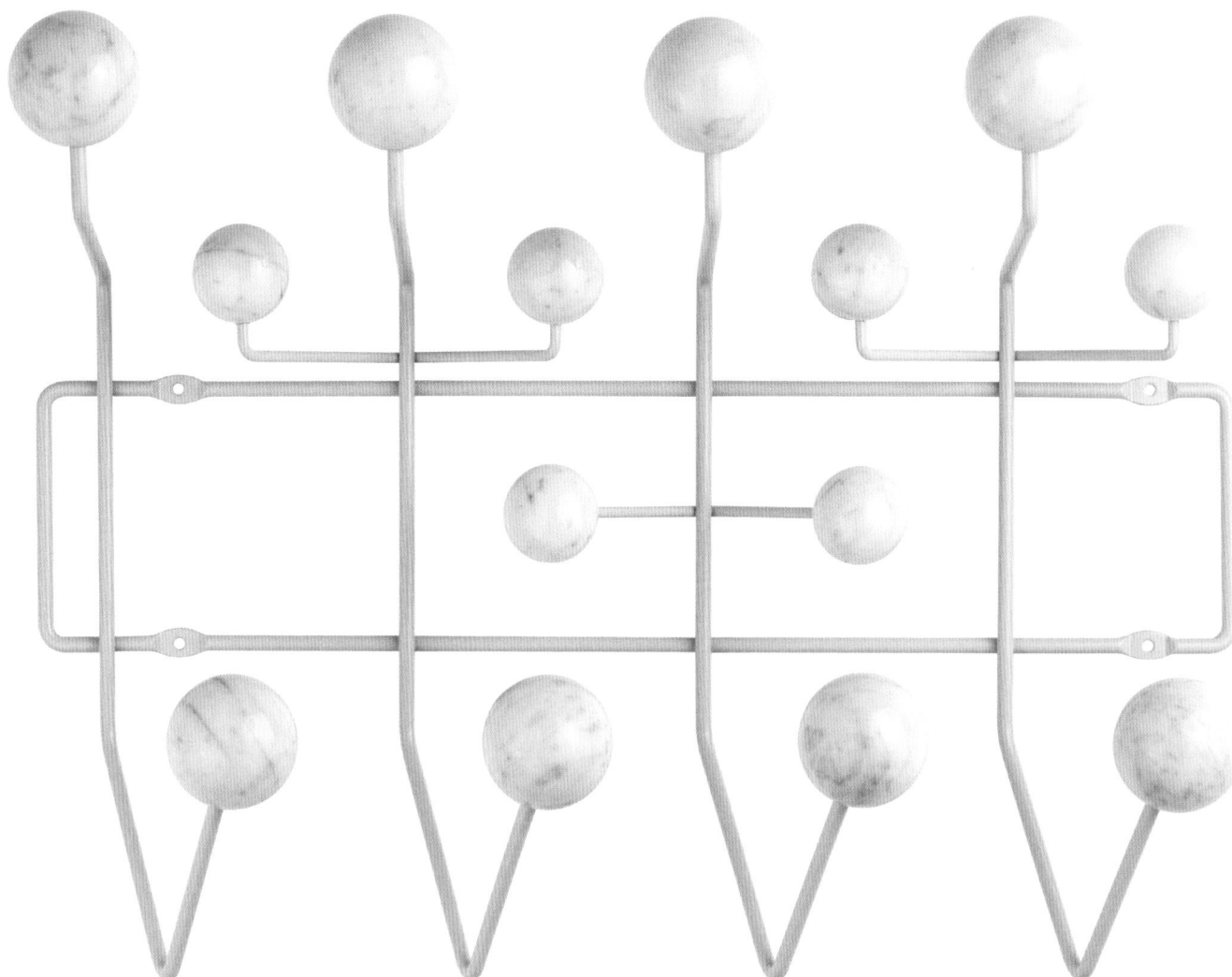

Last but not least, luxury objects can be found in the most unexpected spaces at home, like the entrance hall or a bathroom, and become glamourous additions.

Last but not least finden sich Luxusobjekte an den unerwartetsten Orten im Haus, wie dem Eingangsbereich oder einem Badezimmer, und werden dort zu glamourösen Hinguckern.

VITRA, HANG IT ALL (MARBLE) BY CHARLES AND RAY EAMES
VITRA, HANG IT ALL (MARMOR) VON CHARLES UND RAY EAMES

CLASSICON, USHA UMBRELLA STAND BY ECKART MUTHESIUS
CLASSICON, SCHIRMSTÄNDER USHA VON ECKART MUTHESIUS

> PP. 216-217 S. 216-217
CHRISTIAN LACROIX FOR TOHAA DESIGN, BIRDS SINFONIA COLLECTION
CHRISTIAN LACROIX FÜR TOHAA DESIGN, KOLLEKTION BIRDS SINFONIA

Christian Lacroix

WEBSITES
WEBSEITEN

BRANDS / DESIGNERS
MARKEN / DESIGNER

ALESSI   www.alessi.com

BACCARAT   www.baccarat.com

BOSS   www.hugoboss.com

CASSINA   www.cassina.com

CHOPARD   www.chopard.com

CHRISTIAN LACROIX MAISON

www.christian-lacroix.com

CLASSICON   www.classicon.com

DIOR MAISON   www.dior.com

DOLCE & GABBANA   www.dolcegabbana.com

ETHIMO   www.ethimo.com

EXTETA   www.exteta.it

FENDI CASA   www.fendi.com

FÜRSTENBERG PORZELLAN

www.fuerstenberg-porzellan.com

GEORG JENSEN   www.georgjensen.com

GUCCI   www.gucci.com

KVADRAT   www.kvadrat.dk

LOUIS VUITTON   www.louisvuitton.com

MAISON SCHMIDT   www.home-design.schmidt

MISSONI HOME   www.missoni.com

PAGERIE   www.pagerie.com

PRADA   www.prada.com

RIMOWA   www.rimowa.com

ROSENTHAL   www.rosenthal.de

SMEG   www.smeg.com

SIEGER BY FÜRSTENBERG   www.sieger-germany.com

SUPREME   www.supreme.com

VENINI   www.venini.com

VERSACE   www.versace.com

VITRA   www.vitra.com

ZAHA HADID DESIGN

www.zaha-hadid-design.com

VIRGIL ABLOH   www.virgilabloh.com

ATELIER OÏ   www.atelier-oi.ch

FERNANDO AND HUMBERTO CAMPANA

www.campanas.com.br

CRISTINA CELESTINO   www.cristinacelestino.com

DAVID CHIPPERFIELD   www.davidchipperfield.com

THOMAS DARIEL   www.darielstudio.com

DELFINA DELETTREZ FENDI

www.delfinadelettrez.com

CHARLES AND RAY EAMES   www.eamesoffice.com

FOSTER + PARTNERS   www.fosterandpartners.com

PHILIPPE GARCIA   www.philippegarcia.fr

FRANK GEHRY   www.foga.com

JAIME HAYON   www.hayonstudio.com

SIMON PORTE JACQUEMUS

www.jacquemus.com

DANIEL LIBESKIND   www.libeskind.com

PETER MARINO   www.petermarinoarchitect.com

ALESSANDRO MENDINI   www.ateliermendini.it

SONIA PEDRAZZINI   www.soniapedrazzini.it

GAETANO PESCE   www.gaetanopesce.com

RAW EDGES   www.raw-edges.com

ROLF SACHS   www.rolfsachs.com

PALOMBA SERAFINI   www.palombaserafini.com

RAF SIMONS   www.rafsimons.com

PHILIPPE STARCK   www.starck.fr

STUDIO ADOLINI   www.studioadolini.com

PATRICIA URQUIOLA   www.patriciaurquiola.com

SACHA WALCKHOFF   www.walckhoff.com

MARCEL WANDERS   www.marcelwanders.com

TOKUJIN YOSHIOKA   www.tokujin.com

PIERRE YOVANOVITCH

www.pierreyovanovitch.com

PHOTO CREDITS
BILDNACHWEIS

Front cover © Versace

Pp: 4, 16-17, 55 bottom, 56 top, 58, 59 top, 59 middle, 62 top, 65 bottom, 71, 81 bottom, 87, 88 right, 89 left, 96 bottom, 98-99, 101, 115, 136-139, 164 bottom, 208 bottom © Prada

6-7, 18-19, 75 top,112, 184 top left, 184 top right © FENDI Casa

10 © Christian Lacroix Maison for Vista Alegre. Butterfly Parade Collection by Grégoire Alexandre
11 top © Christian Lacroix Maison for Vista Alegre. Fête Vos Jeux Collection by Philippe Garcia
11 bottom © Christian Lacroix Maison for Designers Guild. Lacroix Stravaganza Collection by Philippe Garcia

12-13, 55 top, 56 bottom, 59 bottom, 62 middle, 81 top, 86 top, 88 left, 90-91, 105 top, 107, 114, 140-141, 185 © DIOR

14-15, 60-61, 69 top, 70, 96 top right, 97, 105 bottom, 108, 130-131, 178 top, 207, 208 top left, 208 top right © Versace

166-169 © Versace Rosenthal

20, 66-67, 69 middle, 75 bottom, 82-83, 86 bottom, 89 right, 94-95, 104, 152, 159, 190-191, 194 © Louis Vuitton Malletier

21, 48-49, 158, 195 © atelier oï
46 © Wang Jian / Courtesy of atelier oï
50 © Kwa Yong Lee / Courtesy of atelier oï

22-23, 69 bottom, 113, 132-133, 184 bottom © Gucci

24-25, 76, 77 bottom, 78-79 © Missoni Home

26 © Photo by Rumman Amin on Unsplash

27 © Photo by Nicolas Weldingh on Unsplash

28, 29 top, 110, 163, 164 top, 174 bottom Baccarat © Palast; 29 bottom, 64 top © Baccarat; 56 middle, 160 bottom, 174 top, 175 Baccarat photo © Laurent Parrault

30-31, 126-127, 142-149 © PAGERIE

35 FENDI, The Happy Room © Cristina Celestino, FENDI

36 Cristina Celestino, Ottavia © FENDI Casa

38-39 Back Home furniture collection by Cristina Celestino for FENDI and FENDI Casa, photo © Omar Sartor

41 © Sacha Walckhoff by Luc Frey
42 top © Christian Lacroix for Galison, Maison de Jeu Notebook by Philippe Garcia
42 bottom © Christian Lacroix Maison for Designers Guild. Lacroix Stravaganza Collection by Philippe Garcia
44 © Christian Lacroix for Big Ben by Neil Bicknell
45 © Christian Lacroix Maison for Roche Bobois by Michel Gaubert

52-53, 72 © Jacquemus, 73 © Jacquemus+Exteta, photo © Théo De Gueltzl

54 © Christian Lacroix for Galison, Playing Cards by Philippe Garcia

57 © Photo by Stephan Coudassot on Unsplash

62 bottom, 106, 120-121 © Chopard

63 © Christian Lacroix for Galison, Backgammon by Philippe Garcia

64 bottom Zaha Hadid Design photo © Karoliina Helosuo, 157 Zaha Hadid Design photo © Rodrigo Carmuega, 206, 209 Zaha Hadid Design photo © Simon Bevan

65 top, 204-205 © Porzellan Manufaktur Nymphenburg

68 © Photo by Tom Morbey on Unsplash

71 Background © Photo by Jonathan Borba on Unsplash

74 © GUBI

77 top, 116-117, 187 © Kvadrat/Raf Simons

80, 109, 111, 153, 160 top left, 160 top right, 162, 178 bottom, 179, 211 bottom © Alessi

84-85 Out-Fit, outdoor gym, design Studio Adolini for Ethimo © Ethimo Photo Courtesy www.ethimo.com

88-89 Background © Photo by Wladislaw Sokolowskij on Unsplash

92 © Photo by Lazar Gugleta on Unsplash

93, 119 © Photo by Joel Muniz on Unsplash

95 Background © Photo by Sam Wermut on Unsplash

96 top left, 123, 128-129, 188-189 © HUGO BOSS

100 © Photo by Maurits Bausenhart on Unsplash

102-103 © Christian Lacroix B5 notebook by Neil Bicknell

118, 124-125, 214 top © Vitra

122 top left and right © Christian Lacroix, Idylle En Vol A5 Notebook by Neil Bicknell
122 bottom © Christian Lacroix, Les Saisons Lacroix by Philippe Garcia

134-135, 154-155, 156 bottom, 210 bottom © sieger design

150-151, 180-181 © Smeg x Dolce & Gabbana / courtesy of s2H communications

156 top, 210 top, 211 top © Venini

161, 202 © Cappellini

165 © Porzellanmanufaktur Fürstenberg, DATUM Foster+Partners

170-173 © Christian Lacroix for Vista Alegre - Caribe collection
176-177 © Christian Lacroix Maison for Maison Schmidt. Prête-Moi Ta Plume and Algae Bloom collections
182 © Christian Lacroix Maison For Designers Guild, Cushions Dame Nature, Le Curieux, Jardin Des Hespérides And Arlecchino Wood
183 © Christian Lacroix Maison For Designers Guild, Cushion Lacroix Paradise By Philippe Garcia

186, 198 © Cassina; 196, 212-213 Cassina photo © Luca Merli; 197 Cassina photo © Valentina Sommariva, 199 Cassina photo © Stefano De Monte

192-193 © FENDI, The Happy Room © Cristina Celestino, FENDI Casa

200-201 © FENDI, The Happy Room, Paravento Screen © Cristina Celestino, FENDI Casa

203 © Georg Jensen

214 bottom © ClassiCon

215, 216-217 © Christian Lacroix for Tohaa Design, Birds Sinfonia Collection

220 © Andrei Antipov/Shutterstock

223 © Photo by Erik Mclean / Pexels

© 2024 teNeues Verlag GmbH

Texts and layout: © Agata Toromanoff, Fancy Books Packaging

Editorial Coordination by Nadine Weinhold, Roman Korn, teNeues Verlag
Production by Sandra Jansen-Dorn, teNeues Verlag
Photo Editing, Color Separation by Jens Grundei, teNeues Verlag
Front Cover Design by Marcus Taeschner

Translation into German by Anna-Saida Jessen
Copyediting by Allison Adelman (English), Nadine Weinhold (German)

ISBN: 978-3-96171-564-0
Library of Congress Number: 2024935912

Printed in Slovakia by Neografia a.s.

MIX
Paper | Supporting
responsible forestry
FSC
www.fsc.org
FSC® C020353

Published by teNeues Publishing Group

teNeues Verlag GmbH
Ohmstraße 8a
86199 Augsburg, Germany

Düsseldorf Office
Waldenburger Straße 13
41564 Kaarst, Germany
e-mail: books@teneues.com

Augsburg/München Office
Ohmstraße 8a
86199 Augsburg, Germany
e-mail: books@teneues.com

Press Department
e-mail: presse@teneues.com

teNeues Publishing Company
350 Seventh Avenue, Suite 301
New York, NY 10001, USA

www.teneues.com

www.teneues.com

https://instagram.com/teneuespublishing

teNeues Publishing Group
Augsburg / München
Berlin
Düsseldorf
London
New York

teNeues